Motorbooks International Illustrated

Illustrated

VOLVO

BUYER'S ★ GUIDE™

John Matras

Motorbooks International
Publishers & Wholesalers

First published in 1993 by Motorbooks International Publishers & Wholesalers, PO Box 2, 729 Prospect Avenue, Osceola, WI 54020 USA

Motorbooks International books are also available at discounts in bulk quantity for industrial or sales-promotional use. For details write to Special Sales Manager at the Publisher's address

Library of Congress Cataloging-in-Publication Data
Matras, John.
    Illustrated Volvo buyer's guide / by John Matras.
        p.   cm.—(Motorbooks International illustrated buyer's guide series)
    Includes index.
    ISBN 0-87938-713-0
    1. Volvo automobile—Purchasing.   I. Title.   II. Series.
    TL215.V65M38   1993
    629.222'2—dc20   92-34618

On the front cover: The 1964 Volvo P1800 owned by William Jeanes. *David Gooley*

Printed and bound in the United States of America

Contents

Acknowledgments

This book would have been impossible for me to write without the enthusiastic assistance of many individuals and I'd like to thank as many as possible. Bob Austin, Volvo's communication director, and Michael Guerra, of Volvo public relations, were particularly helpful with data and old publicity photos, going above and beyond the call of duty.

Individuals who contributed to this book in various ways include, in alphabetical order: Charles and Eileen Baldwin, Mike Bernard, Chris Buscher, Garland Culpepper, Paul Curran, Dennis Dailey, Robert Foltz, Richard Gordon, Michael Hamilton, Scott Hart, John Heilig, David Humphreys, Tom Jugus, Michael Leslie, Duane Matejka, Pete Neilsen, Bob Newman, Ray Parsons, Ron and Brenda Powell, Paul Provencher, Larry Rembold, Ron Sessions, Jerry Sira, Bob Stein, Jonathan Stein, Jim Stem, Boyd Swartz, John Switzer, and David and Deborah Woods. And thanks to all the Volvo enthusiasts who keep the meaning in "I roll."

Special thanks to my wife Mary Ann for her encouragement over the years, and to our daughters Mandy, Cari, and Katie.

And to my biggest fan and best and most resolute friend, John Matras, my father. Godspeed, Dad.

Introduction

Volvos aren't like Ferraris. You won't make a fortune by collecting them. On the other hand, the hobby won't cost you a fortune either. Car and part costs are mostly reasonable, the effect of the limited supply of some rare pieces being moderated by a less than overwhelming demand, as well as the big money off chasing more exotic toys, such as the aforementioned Ferraris. As a Volvo staffer once confessed, Volvos are cars one doesn't lust after, but that one can love.

Be that as it may, the absence of outrageous price tags on Volvos means that the collector needn't be afraid to play with his or her toy. You can drive them to meets, not trailer them. People have been known to use Ferraris as their retirement plan, but anybody who plans to do so with a Volvo had best be prepared to live frugally.

That doesn't mean you can't spend a fortune restoring a Volvo. It costs about the same to straighten a fender on a Volvo as it does on a Ferrari, although you are more likely to find new-old-stock parts or good salvage yard parts for a Volvo—any Volvo—than a Ferrari. Just the same, it's always a good idea, when looking for a project car, to start with one in better shape because the price differential between an average and poor car will be less than the cost of bringing a poor car up to average. The total cost of an average car plus restoration will be less than for a cheaper poor-condition car with more expensive restoration. Of course, there are a lot of reasons for automotive restoration, so

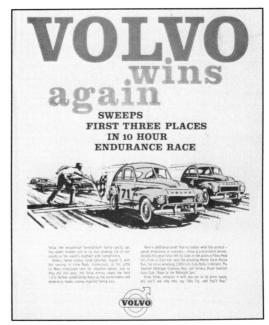

Volvo emphasized not only its durability but speed in this ad that ran in November 1958.

don't let this discourage you if you're set on saving some poor, lost Volvo. But as Aesop said, look before you leap.

There are three major parts to this *Illustrated Volvo Buyer's Guide.* First is the prewar history of Volvo. Unfortunately, precious few Volvos were built before World War II in the United States and sorry, but I can't write an entire guide for buying those few cars. But those cars, even if never offered commercially in the United States, are the predecessors of every modern Volvo.

The next section deals with collectible Volvos in the United States. Because of its intended audience, the book considers primarily those models and versions that were sold in the North American market. It notes the models and changes made over the years, discusses advantages and disadvantages among models and years, and provides advice on "what to look for."

It should be noted that up through the mid to late sixties, many cars were registered as the year they were sold. Thus a car that remained on a dealer's lot over the model year change may carry a later year registration than the actual build date of the car. Therefore, the text refers to these earlier Volvos by letter series rather than strictly by model year to avoid confusion.

The third section brings Volvo up to date, although there's no clear demarcation— one man's used car is another man's collectible. And the more desirable the model was when it was new, the sooner it will be considered collectible. The modestly named Matras Curve, however, holds that cars typically bottom out in value at about age twenty. Anything over twenty years old begins increasing in value, if only because the slings and arrows of day-to-day life have changed something that was common into something rare and interesting. Cars such as the 242GT or 262C, however, will be ahead of the curve because they were more desirable and less common in the first place.

Section three follows the development of late-model Volvos, noting when worthwhile accessories or more horsepower(!) came, making particular models more desirable than others and simplifying that search for the good, used Volvo. And considering how Volvos last, today's used car—if it's a Volvo—will still be around when it's a collectible.

When looking for a car that's already a collectible, one should realize that the low-mileage car so prized in other circles doesn't necessarily carry the same premium in Volvoland. In fact, high-mileage cars—in good condition—are prized and celebrated at Volvo gatherings. The only meet I've ever attended where a "highest odometer reading" trophy was awarded was a Volvo meet. Yes, they really do compare odometers and, like some other things, bigger is better— although not necessarily worth more when the car is sold. . . . Volvo also awards grille badges for vehicles that have passed mileage milestones.

Cars with documented racing history will be worth more, as well. Vintage racing has become popular of late, but few vintage competition Volvos have been out on the track. Volvos make an excellent vintage racer for the individual who doesn't care to jeopardize (again) the kids' college fund with an expensive exotic out on the track. The relative unburstability of the Volvo drivetrain is another plus. You don't have to worry about some overstressed Italian widget ruining your racing weekend and/or putting the family on a diet of peanut butter sandwiches. The fact that Volvo has made competition parts for years is another advantage. There's no question of sanctioning bodies allowing modifications if they were available from the factory for any given year.

Of course, one of the best parts of Volvomania is the people. There are few snobs, but mostly they are just folks who've found a good way to have fun with cars. Three major clubs exist (see appendices), full of people willing and eager to help share The Volvo Experience. Arguably more Volvos than Ferraris have been restored by their owners, so for the hands-on sort there's always someone around to assist.

Local and national meets are good places to look into the hobby, make contacts, and possibly find a car or spread the word that you're interested. Swap meets at Volvo events also bring vendors of Volvo parts. You may not get the bargain that you might from the Hershey or Carlisle vendor's grab bag of mixed parts, but you will probably more than make it up in time spent.

Volvos aren't Ferraris, not even the 1800 series. But that doesn't mean you can't have just as much fun with a sexy Swede as an Italian exotic. And anyway, as the old P1800 ad said, "What's it like to own a $10,000 car? Find out for $3995." The prices aren't the same anymore, but the idea remains.

Investment Ratings

★★★★★—The best of the collectible Volvos. As with most collectibles, value increases with age, scarcity, and desirability. There are no more than a handful of prewar Volvos in all of North America and not that many in Europe. A restored example won't be cheap, and an unrestored one is unlikely to be found in a barn, and even then restoring it will be difficult and expensive. But then, scarcity has its own rewards.

This category also includes the P1900, of which only a few survive in the United States, but which may be still lodged in the back of someone's garage.

Also included are the 1800 series, whose sexy curves push it to the top rank. Auction impresario Rick Cole put the 1800 on his Gold List of cars expected to increase in value. Cars are still relatively available, however, so prices are mostly under $20,000 for even the best of the best. Mostly early and later (pre-smog) cars qualify for five stars, the former for scarcity and the latter because they come with more horsepower. The ES has a cult of its own, however.

★★★★—A notch down from the most collectible are the slightly newer, slightly more available, and slightly less desirable models—though not necessarily all of the above. Thus the PV444 and PV544 fall in this range. The 123GT belongs here as well, if not a star or half-star higher. Don't expect to find these cars in anything but *Hemmings* or similar classifieds.

★★★—These cars are still excellent values, hardly common and still desirable. The 120 series typifies the next ranking, with more available to choose from than the PV444 and PV544. Within the 120 line, the wagons have developed something of a cult, and period-modified two-doors can carry a premium as well.

The 142E and 242GT are both desirable, though not quite so old. You might see one of this latter pair in the local classifieds, possibly at a good price from a "civilian" who thinks of it as "just an old car."

The 164 and 262C/Coupe have enough of a cult following and are scarce enough to qualify here as well.

★★—Fun-to-drive cars, some with investment potential but not old enough to be collectible, and older cars that don't have the panache of special models. The 240 Turbos of the early eighties belong here as do most of the 140s, although the 140, especially the first series, is becoming old enough to start collecting nostalgia points. They're the last of the carbureted Volvos and the first Volvo for many an aging baby boomer!

★—These are common, readily available cars. The 700 and 900 series are included completely, as well as many 240s. That doesn't mean these are necessarily cheaper than cars with higher collector status. For example, a used year-old 960 will cost more than almost any older collectible Volvo, but don't expect its value to go up for a long time (unless Volvo goes out of business, and don't hold your breath on that!). The 900s, 700s, and late 240s are still "used cars." On the other hand, prices for two star or higher cars should hold their own or appreciate, all other things being equal.

For the newer cars, the Volvo-engined models have more potential collectible status, if only because the V-6 is so despised among Volvo enthusiasts. (That's subject to change, of course. Maybe after they become rare. . . ?) The exception to this are the Bertone Coupes of 1978 through 1981 and 1987 through 1991. The latter came with the special high-output turbocharged four as well as the V-6; the four is preferred. In its final year, 1991, the Coupe came only with the four and only 400 were imported into the United States. For a late-model exotic Volvo, it's the best choice.

Among older models, cars with options or genuine Volvo accessories will carry a premium. On the other hand, modified cars won't necessarily lose value for not being authentic. In fact, if modified with genuine Volvo Competition Service parts or other period-correct parts, value should increase, especially for a well-done or original modification. You should be able to get your money out of a late-model modified car from the right buyer—though don't expect the salesperson at the used car lot to do handsprings because you put accessory antiroll bars on your 740. Putting a V-8 in your Volvo will make it more fun to drive, but again, don't expect it to do much for the value.

As emission regulations continue to stiffen, you may find that your car is illegal in some jurisdictions, even though it doesn't pollute. And that won't help its value.

Authentic Volvo accessories are valued commodities, so an item such as a roof rack for a 122S wagon is valuable alone or with a car.

A number of Volvos were raced, if not extensively, then with intensity. But few Volvos have been seen in vintage racing. Considering durability and the relatively low cost of cars and parts, a Volvo is a good way to go vintage racing. Requirements vary by sanctioning body, but the PV444, PV544, the 1800 series, and the 140 series all qualify somewhere or other. Don't chop up or part out that car with documentable racing history. Sell it to someone who will take it vintage racing, or do it yourself.

Ratings given to cars not imported to the United States after 1970—for example, the 66, 340, and 360 series, and the 400 series—reflect more of their international status. You can't have these cars here legally, except with special, hard-to-get permits. If, on the other hand, you had one in the United States, it would be a sure crowd-gatherer at Volvo or other imported car meets. But keeping it, in this increasingly regulated country, will be more and more difficult, particularly if you want to register it. With the smog police moving in, these make a particularly risky investment.

The advantage to Volvo collecting is that high mileage isn't by itself a disadvantage. Volvo owners wear their car's accumulated miles with pride. As such, they aren't afraid to drive them, and that's where the value of a Volvo lies. If you just want to invest, check out mutual funds or certificates of deposit. Leave the Volvos to those who will drive them.

Chapter 1

Prewar Volvos 1927-1949

American Theme, Swedish Variations

★★★★★	OV4/PV4
★★★★★	PV651/PV652
★★★★★	PV653/PV654/PV655; TR675-679
★★★★★	PV658/PV659
★★★★★	PV656/PV657/TR701-704
★★★★★	PV36
★★★★★	PV51/PV52
★★★★★	PV53/PV54/PV55/PV56/ PV57
★★★★★	PV801/PV802
★★★★★	PV60

"I roll" is a wonderfully appropriate name for an automobile. Change it to Latin and it's even better: *Volvo*. The name has been on cars since 1927, durable as the cars that wore it.

The term didn't originate with the automobile, however, but with the Swedish bearing manufacturer Svenska Kullagerfabriken (SKF), which trademarked the name for use on deep-groove ball bearings, a simpler version of the spherical ball bearings SKF manufactured. The name was used from about 1915 to 1919.

Its use on motor vehicles didn't occur until Assar Gabrielsson and Gustaf Larson joined efforts to create a Swedish-built automobile. Gabrielsson was sales manager for SKF where Larson was an engineer. It was outside of the factory, however, that the concept and building of the automobile took place. In August of 1924, the two men signed an agreement to begin "large-scale car manufacture" no later than January 1, 1928.

A month later, design work was begun on the new Swedish car in Larson's apartment in Stockholm. For a long time the car was referred to as the GL (for Gustav Larson) or as the Larson. Meanwhile, Gabrielsson set about raising the capital—mostly borrowed from banks but also from his own funds—to build prototypes.

The decision to produce the prototypes was made in September 1925, with original-design parts to be supplied by (mostly) Swedish firms. Ten cars—one sedan and nine open touring cars—were to be built, the

A later prototype of Volvo's first model undergoes testing—as does the stamina of the driver! *Volvo*

first one completed about June 1926. It was this car that was driven by Gabrielsson and Larson to SKF headquarters for a meeting with the company's board of directors. Two days after the meeting, a contract was drawn up and signed. SKF would revive AB Volvo and install Assar Gabrielsson as managing director on the first day of 1927. SKF loaned the new car manufacturer 2 million kroner, with additional financing coming from public funds.

OV4/PV4 Series

The first production Volvo was put on public display in Stockholm on April 14, 1927.

9

The OV4 was Volvo's first car, beginning production in 1927. *Volvo*

The PV4 was the sedan version of the OV4. PV indicated *Person Vagn*, while OV stood for *Oppen Vagn*, or open car. *Volvo*

It was a ruggedly built open tourer on solid axles front and rear, powered by a side-valve four-cylinder engine displacing 1940cc and rated at 28bhp at 2000rpm. It was built on this design, partly because several of the engineers developing it had worked in the United States, and partly because 90 percent of the cars sold in Sweden at the time were American. That was because American cars suited Swedish conditions, which resembled those in the United States—primarily unpaved roads. Volvos placed function over style.

The 1929 PV651 was the first Volvo six-cylinder car. Styling was very American. *Volvo*

From the beginning, all Volvos were marked with a diagonal band across the radiator on which the traditional Swedish symbol for iron was stamped, which serendipitously was the international sign for man. It was simple and direct and immediately identifiable while unequivocally communicating the message that Volvos were strong and robust. An enameled oval inscribed with the Volvo name was placed on the radiator header tank.

The open tourer, selling for 4,800 kroner, was called the OV4 (for *Oppen Vagn,* or open car), and the PV4 sedan (for *Person Vagn*) followed in July. The 4 stood for the number of cylinders. By mid-1929, when production of the model was ended, 205 touring cars, 443 sedans, and 251 Special sedans had been built, along with seventy cars specially made for the Swedish post office and twenty-seven chassis to be bodied by outside concerns.

PV651/PV652 Series

Though it wouldn't go on sale until three months later, the first six-cylinder Volvo debuted in April 1929, following the trend to six-cylinder engines in the United States. The new Volvo was called the PV651, which stood for Private Car, six-cylinder, five-passenger, series one. It was a great advance from the four-cylinder cars. Not only did it look bet-

The PV653/PV654 was introduced in August 1933. Note the wire instead of wood artillery wheels, a more American-inspired styling. *Volvo*

ter—the longer hood was more attractive than the stubby four-cylinder's—but the new car was longer and wider, with more interior room thanks to a dropped center section in the frame and a hypoid bevel rear end that lowered the driveshaft.

The six-cylinder engine, which resembled the Continental engine made in the United States, displaced 3010cc and produced 55hp at 3000rpm, the higher engine speed allowed by a beefy seven-main-bearing crankshaft that was balanced statically and dynamically. The compression ratio was 5.1:1, higher than the fours, and a water pump was used instead of the thermosyphon system of the older engine. A three-speed gearbox came from Warner Gear in the United States.

Volvo sold some 1,383 vehicles in 1929, including the leftover fours. More importantly, the company showed its first, if meager, profit during that year.

The PV652 appeared early in 1930, and with only minor visual changes was difficult to tell from its predecessor. However, a Stromberg carburetor with an accelerator pump replaced the previous model's Solex, and Lockheed hydraulic brakes were fitted. The engine was updated a year later, being bored out to 3366cc and rated at 65hp. Though a four-speed was adopted for a short time, a freewheeling three-speed synchronized on second and third replaced it.

PV653/PV654/PV655 Series

The PV653 (standard) and PV654 (Deluxe) were introduced in August 1933. Again, America provided the inspiration for the two model lines. The PV653 was available only in dark blue, while the PV654 added maroon, chestnut brown, and possibly, sand brown, though for minimal extra cost, any color could be specified. The PV654 also had a more lavishly upholstered interior, two spare wheels instead of one (one mounted in each front fender), two chrome-plated horns, twin brake and taillights (including a back-up light), and foldable rear seat armrests and passenger straps.

Both models received the same mechanical upgrades, including a stronger X-braced frame (as per the better American practice) and more sound and vibration damping. Wheel diameter decreased from 19in to 17in, following the international trend to bigger tires and smaller wheels. Front fenders received more wraparound to reduce splash and the radiator was slightly raked, though one had to know to look for the changes. Volvo pointed out in its catalog that the company had no desire to change every year for the sake of change. . . .

Volvo also offered a chassis-only version of the PV653/PV654 designated, likely enough, the PV655. Taxi versions, TR675–679, differed mainly in wheelbase and fittings and were available from 1934–1935.

PV658/PV659 Series

The PV658 and PV659, standard and Deluxe models respectively, appeared in 1935. Although still recognizably Volvos, the noticeably sloped radiator *cum* grille with a slight vee shape marked the new models. The engine was enlarged, this time bored to a 3670cc displacement. That, along with valve diameter changes and a compression ratio increase to 6.1:1 bumped the rated power to 80hp.

Model numbers PV656 and PV657 were reserved for chassis-only, the latter for a long-wheelbase ambulance version. Taxi applications were designated TR701–704, for some

reason abandoning the established numbering scheme.

PV36 Series

The PV36, also released in 1935, not only altered the method of model designation, but was a completely new model except for the engine. The "modern" streamlined bodyshell was so similar in appearance to the DeSoto and Chrysler Airflow models of 1934, suggestions have been made that Volvo somehow knew what was coming.

Built on a conventional frame, the PV36 had independent front suspension with coil springs; the rear suspension still had a live axle on leaf springs but with an antiroll bar added. Steel artillery-style 16in wheels were fitted with 6.50 section tires.

There was no differentiation between standard and Deluxe models as every PV36 received premium fittings. The model run was limited to 500 cars though; as with Chrysler, the avant-garde styling proved a hard sell, the last cars not being sold until 1938. Still, the PV36 outsold the PV658/PV659.

PV51/PV52 Series

Both models were overshadowed, however, by the PV51, introduced at the very end of 1936. Less expensive than the PV36, at

The radiator was raked and a vee'd grille installed, distinguishing the PV658/PV659 from its predecessors when introduced in 1935. *Volvo*

The PV36 of 1935 was nicknamed the Carioca, probably after the South American dance popular at the time. Chrysler Airflow influence is more than evident. *Volvo*

5,800 versus 8,500 kroner, the PV51 was also less radically styled, with a more conventional front end although the roofline and tail section bore strong resemblance to the PV36. For the first time, the roof was all steel, without the cutout that had to be covered with fabric, but a solid-beam front axle was reintroduced, being more economical than the independent system. Front and rear anti-roll bars were used, however.

The designation PV51 is thought to have been inspired by the Swedish idiom "5–1," which somehow means "right on target." For some, however, it hit too low: one windshield wiper, no armrests on the doors, and so forth. So Volvo created the PV52, released in early 1937, which was more completely and lavishly equipped, but otherwise the same car. Many buyers specified 52 equipment (wipers and heater) for their PV51, however,

so such trappings don't necessarily mean the car is the more expensive model.

A PV51 Special moved the spare tire from the deck lid to the trunk floor, eliminating the continental bulge for a sleeker appearance. This was followed by a PV52 Special.

PV53–PV57 Series

In the fall of 1938, Volvo conducted a new-model introduction—expressly to be more like American car makers—launching no fewer than four new models, five counting the chassis-only version. These were all variations of an update of the PV51–52 series, based on the same chassis except with a tubular cross-member up front instead of a complicated (and more expensive) sheet-steel pressing. The front suspension was softened, the steering system modified, and

The PV51/PV52 got a one-piece windshield and more conventional styling than their predecessors. *Volvo*

13

The PV60 was Volvo's first post-World War II car, though in spirit it was a prewar model, with a nose lifted from the 1939 Pontiac. Most were built in 1949–1950, although the smaller PV444 was the first true postwar Volvo. *Volvo*

the compression ratio raised, although rated horsepower stayed the same. More obvious were the styling changes, primarily a more pointed, almost American-style grille.

The model variations involved fittings, both standard and Deluxe, and trunk type, but the cars were otherwise identical. The standard PV53 had the spare in the trunk lid, while the PV54 carried it inside of a bustle-shaped trunk. The Deluxe versions of these bodystyles were designated PV55 and PV56 respectively, and the chassis-only PV57.

A new taxi was introduced in 1938 as well, and called the PV801 and PV802, respectively with and without a partition. Both were eight-seaters (three were folding seats) and stylistically similar to their private-duty siblings with a pointed nose, but different grille shape.

PV60/PV61 Series

The outbreak of war in September 1939 interrupted Volvo's plans to introduce the PV60 in 1940; in fact, this larger, more American-style car, which some have compared to the 1939 Pontiac, didn't start production until December 1946. The PV60 incorporated independent front suspension and a live axle on leaf springs, but the engine was a further refinement of the side-valve six, now producing 90hp, thanks to a compression ratio of 6.5:1. The three-speed gearbox had an automatic overdrive, and for the first time, Volvo put the shift lever on the steering column, as had become popular in, yes, the United States.

Volvo made some 3,000 PV60s between 1946 and 1949, and about 500 PV61s, as the chassis-only was known. Although no PV60 series automobiles, other than prototypes, were made until after the war's end, it's fair to include the model in the prewar group, considering its heritage and the clean break in design signaled by the PV444, which is truly the first postwar Volvo.

★★★★	PV444
★★★★	PV544
★★★★★$^{1}/_{2}$	PV445/Duett/210

PV444 and PV544 1944-1965

The Swedish Immigrant

Even Volvo's own advertisements compared the look of the Volvo PV444 to the 1940 Ford. But not without reason. Volvo had employed one Helmer Petterson as a consultant when the decision was made in 1943 to design a car to build after the war. Petterson, though a native Swede, had worked for the Excelsior motorcycle company in Chicago during the 1920s and for GM and Ford dealers in Sweden in the 1930s, as well as on several automotive projects. It was Petterson's idea that Volvo should build a small car; Gabrielsson, having been convinced of the notion, appointed Petterson to the project that would lead to the

Early European PV444 had a different grille, "scooped" front bumper, and lacked side trim of cars exported to the United States. *Volvo*

The definitive PV444 as exported to the United States. American rail bumpers were designed for American parking habits. And yes, whitewalls are period correct for 1958. Owner is Boyd Swartz.

PV444 and its successor the PV544, as well as the station wagon PV445 and Duett/210.

PV444 Series

Although novel powertrains were considered, including front-wheel-drive and two-stroke and horizontal inline engines, Larson deemed these too far afield for Volvo. A thoroughly conventional vertical, inline four-cylinder engine with overhead valves driving the rear wheels would prove to be the eventual configuration. However, unit-body construction—like the 1939 German Hanomag the engineering staff bought to study—would be a relatively avant-garde feature of the PV444, especially for conservative Volvo.

The body shape, on the other hand, was unabashedly derivative. Petterson openly ad-

PV444 Series Production

Model	Series	Production Dates	Number Built
PV444	A	1944-1950	11,804
	AS	1950	700
	B	9/1950-9/1951	4,500
	BS	9/1950-9/1951	3,000
	C	6/1951-8/1952	3,500
	CS	6/1951-8/1952	4,500
	D	8/1952-4/1953	3,500
	DS	8/1952-4/1953	5,500
	E	4/1953-12/1954	14,350
	ES	4/1953-12/1954	17,599
	H/HS	12/1954-12/1955	29,046
	K/KS	12/1955-12/1956	33,918
	L/LS	1/1957-1958	64,087
		Total:	196,004

mitted that Pontiac and Ford inspired the body contours that, if not as exciting as the better Italian designs at least wasn't as offensive as some of the worst.

The model designation never received any official explanation other than in *Rattan*, the Volvo customer magazine, which noted in 1945: "There is speculation as to why Volvo's little peace car is known as the PV444. Agile minds have concluded that it must be because the car has four wheels and was publicly launched in Autumn '44. The explanation is said to be that the car is a four-seater and has a 40-horsepower, four cylinder engine."

Production didn't immediately follow the introduction, however. A nationwide strike broke out in February 1945, and then a shortage of supplies, particularly sheet steel (a common problem for all auto makers after the war), and developmental teething problems delayed actual production until February 1947. When car making finally got under way, Volvo quickly began setting records for car building, with 2,988 cars (mostly PV444s) built in 1948, the most it had ever built. In 1949, Volvo built more cars than trucks and buses for the first time.

Volvo improved the PV444 with running changes during production, including a Special version (designated PV444S) with better trim and a dove gray external color. Black was also available to the Special buyer, but Volvo historian Bjorn-Eric Lindh points out that few opted for it, mainly because they didn't want to look like they had bought the cheaper version.

In 1950, the PV444B was introduced, with minor external and internal trim and operational changes. Again, a Special version with upgraded trim was offered and called the PV444BS. The earlier model, retroactively designated the A series, had seen a power increase from 40 or 42hp (depending on which of Volvo's figures you believe) to 44hp.

A most distinctive feature of the B series was a T-shaped direction indicator on the middle of the roof. Officially called a Fixlight, Swedes quickly took to calling it the "cuckoo on the roof." It was eliminated by popular demand by summer 1952, replaced with

Rear view of PV444 shows rounded contours and smaller rear window than PV544.

1957 PV444

Dimensions

Wheelbase	102.4in
Track	50.8/51.6in
Length	175in
Width	62.5in
Height	61.5in
Weight	2,120lb

Engine

Type	Ohv I-4
Bore & stroke	2.95x3.15in (75x80mm)
Displacement	86.3ci (1414cc)
Compression	7.8:1
Fuel delivery	Two SU (1V)
Horsepower	70bhp @ 5500rpm
Torque	76lb-ft @ 3000rpm

Chassis and Drivetrain

Layout, engine/drivetrain	F/R
Frame/body	Unit steel
Transmission	Three-speed manual
Rear axle ratio	4.55:1
Suspension, F/R	A-arm/live axle
Tires	5.90-15
Brakes	Drum/drum

Performance

0-60mph	14.5sec
1/4 mile	20.3sec @ N/A
Fuel mileage	25–32mpg
Top speed	90mph

flashing indicators on the door pillars.

The C series replaced the B series in June 1951, and like its predecessors, the standard model was available only in black, the Special in dove gray. Fifteen-inch wheels replaced sixteen-inchers, while wheel bolts went from four to five.

The PV444D and DS came out in August 1952, featuring a higher-capacity generator and a factory-optional heater. Incredibly, even in Sweden heaters were not standard equipment; in fact, they were only available as an aftermarket item. Not surprisingly, dealers equipped most cars with them. A metallic maroon became an optional color for the PV444DS though as with many reds, it proved problematical.

PV444E and ES versions ran from April 1953 to December 1954, with trim and electrical system changes and, on later cars, a Zenith rather than Carter carburetor. And finally, heaters became standard equipment.

Volvo inexplicably skipped F and G model designations, going directly to H and HS in December 1954. Perhaps the jump was justified by the extensive changes in the new model: a bigger windshield and rear window, smaller pillars, and relocated taillights, as well as a number of other, minor modifications.

An Export model, a stripper with painted bumpers, austere interiors, and no oil filter, was prepared, and though it did poorly in Sweden because of a minimal price differential after a heater was added back in, sales in South America as well as Belgium, Denmark, and Norway were sufficient to keep the model in the line-up.

Exports to the United States began not with the stripped Export model, but with an even more upscale PV444HS equipped with a 70hp "sports" engine (called the B14A), fortified with twin SU sidedraft carburetors, a different camshaft, and larger intake valves. (Because of US tariff considerations, the sports engine could not be offered in Sweden, though Swedish enthusiasts tried everything to get one.)

The first shipment of Volvos went to California, Volvo correctly identifying Los Angeles as a trend-setting area. American-bound cars had the door-pillar-mounted turn indicators replaced by turn signals on the front fenders and, in deference to the American park-by-ear habit, "American rails"—tubular extra bumper bars—were added to the front and rear bumpers.

Volvo again skipped letters, there being no I or J models, going directly to K and KS (1955–1957). A special white model was introduced for America. Called the California, it featured Sunshine Yellow and black upholstery and a black steering wheel. The biggest difference between the K and KS and their

PV444 has full instrumentation except for tachometer; also has lots of chrome.

The bulletproof B16 of the PV444 sports a pair of SU carburetors. Object in foreground is heater blower!

predecessors was a more powerful engine for the home market, which still couldn't have the 70hp sports engine.

The eighth and final iterations of the PV444 were the L and LS versions. These were the best of the 444s, with a completely new B16A engine. Displacing about 1580cc, the domestic model went to 60bhp, while the sport version (B16B) for America was rated at 85bhp. Other mechanical changes included a revised shift lever with reduced vibration and noise, a quieter exhaust system, and electric windshield wipers instead of the older vacuum-powered type.

The L Series PV444 could be easily identified by a finer mesh grille (home-market cars got a gold vee on the grille and trunk lid) and repositioned brightmetal trim, from just under the side windows to below the character line in the side sheet metal. Seatbelt mountings were provided, though belts themselves were an option that many dealers installed on their own.

A four-speed gearbox was added for the L Series (only for export models—not Export models, as the slow-selling stripper had been discontinued) as a running change. The four-speed was doubly welcome, as it was all-synchro, rather than synchronized on the top two, as was the three-speed.

PV544 Series Production

Model	Series	Production Dates	Number Built
PV544	A	8/1958-8/1960	99,495
	B	8/1960-8/1961	34,600
	C	8/1961-8/1962	37,900
	D	8/1962-8/1963	27,100
	E	8/1963-8/1964	24,200
	F	8/1964-8/1965	17,300
	G	8/1965-10/1966	3,400
			Total: 243,996

PV544 Series

The PV444L may have been the end of the 444 generation, but by no means was it the end of the 1941 Ford-look Volvo. Despite the debut of the Volvo Amazon 120 Series in 1956, finally reaching the United States in 1959, the PV444 was extensively updated and improved, and in August 1958, it was reintroduced in Sweden as the PV544. US introduction followed in April 1959. It made good sense for Volvo, which had fully amortized the tooling by then, and allowed the PV544 to be offered at a lower price than the new 120.

The PV544 was easily recognizable to those who knew that a curved single-piece windshield (12 percent larger) replaced the split screen of the PV444 and that, instead of

Most PV444s have small, round taillights like these, though some changeover cars have the larger PV544 rear lamps.

The PV544 was labeled with a shield-type badge on the side of the cowl.

small round taillights, the PV544 had larger, vertical units that incorporated a reflector. The list of enhancements included narrower A-pillars and windshield washer nozzles that became standard equipment—though the washer pumps themselves were an optional extra.

The interior saw a rear seat 17cm wider, which allowed the car to be technically called a five-seater in Sweden, and rear seatbelt attachments were standard equipment. The front seats were thinner for more legroom in back. The driver got a band-type speedometer, which was highly criticized by the American enthusiast press (where does one read the speed—point, middle, or heel of the leading edge of the indicator?) and a "safety" steering wheel with a recessed hub. Also new on the US-destined PV544s (and domestic Special I models) were opening rear side windows.

New Gearboxes and the B18

The PV544B appeared in 1960, featuring new three- and four-speed gearboxes, both fully synchronized. The four-speed was designed from the start as a four-speed, rather than as a three-speed with the fourth ratio cobbled in.

The big change came with the PV544C in 1961 (1962 model year in the United States) with the addition of a larger engine, the B18. The B18, of course, was the motivator of the P1800 introduced in 1960. Displacing 1778cc and producing 90bhp in American PV544 trim, it was bolted to a four-speed transmission of Volvo design (planned from the start to be a four-speed, rather than a converted three-speed as the earlier four gearbox had been).

The front suspension and steering was improved and the electrical system went to twelve volts. Externally, the traditional circle-

The one-piece windshield is a quick identifier of the PV544 from the front. Note the new ventilated steel wheels. Owner is Garland Culpepper.

Larger, oval taillights are the spotter's guide to the PV544 if matched with the bigger rear window. Sport emblem indicated the ninety-horse engine on the home market, although all US-bound cars got this twin-carb motor.

Volvo is **the** sports car, **family style**

Volvo proves that the true economy car can still have the essential sports car qualities of power and maneuverability and quick response.

With its superlative 85 h.p. engine, Volvo performs with a get-up-and-go that other cars with more cylinders find difficult to match. That's why Volvo has won such wide respect in major automotive competitions throughout the world. When you buy Volvo, you buy a *complete* family sports car—in quality, performance, equipment, and economy. These are the qualities that make Volvo *the* sports car, family style. Visit your Volvo dealer—he'll gladly give you a test drive.

Sold and serviced by a network of dealers coast-to-coast. Ask about our European Delivery Plan. Write Volvo Import, Inc., Englewood Cliffs, N. J.

Symbol of superb Swedish engineering and craftsmanship

AUTOMOBILES · TRUCKS · MARINE and INDUSTRIAL ENGINES

With the economy car in vogue in 1960, Volvo increased frugality and responsibility in its advertisements.

with-arrow Volvo logo on the grille was replaced with a red-lettered B-18 badge so cars ahead could see what was gaining on them.

PV544 sales declined as production of the 120 Series increased. Nevertheless, Volvo continued to improve the model. The Model D in 1962 got new hubcaps and improved rustproofing. A new roofliner and green instrument lighting went into the 1963 Model E, while the PV544F got new emblems for the sides and trunk lid, and silver-painted wheels with oval cooling holes and smaller hubcaps.

In August 1965 the PV544G was introduced, a new rating of 95bhp being the major change.

Production ceased in October 1965, however, and of a total of 243,996 PV544s, only 3,400 were the Model G. From introduction in 1944 to demise in 1966, Volvo made 440,000 PV444/544s, far more than any model the car maker had produced before and for a longer period than Volvo has produced since.

What to Look For

Sentiment aside, 1962 and later is the better buy in the 444/544 Series. Parts are becoming difficult, if not impossible, to find for the B16 and B14 engines. Water pumps, fuel pumps, and parts for the SU HS4 carburetors can be particularly hard to come by. Some owners have simply given up and replaced the B16 of 444s or early 544s with the B18 and saved themselves the search but, of course, ruining the vehicle's authenticity.

The short front shock absorbers on both 444s and 544s are also hard to get; generic units can be used at the rear. On the other hand, more and more reproduction parts are being made for these cars all the time. It may be easier to restore them as they get older.

The B18 also came with a twelve-volt electrical system, which means better light-

Rugged B18 fits in the PV544 engine compartment with room to spare.

Starsky and Hutch would be proud of this Duett van seen in Sweden. Large-slot wheels and parking-lamp location identify it as a P210 rather than a 445.

ing, easier starting, and all the other reasons that the world gave up six-volt electrical systems. The carburetor and choke linkage were improved on the B18 and became easier to adjust.

The four-wheel drum brakes will likely need to be overhauled if they haven't been already; the four-wheel drums, if they aren't in top condition, can be dodgy, and even when they are in good shape they're hard to get right. Brake shoes can be hard to find.

Rust is a problem on any car in the northern rust belt, but at least the 444/544 doesn't hide its rust problems. Unrestored

What's a Duett Traktor? Swedish teens can drive farm implements at 15, so they customize Duetts (even 122s or 142s) to a pickup-truck configuration, which counts under Swedish rules even if the owner doesn't live on a farm. (American-style pickups are otherwise uncommon in Sweden.) Not all are as wild as this one, but American car magazines are available on larger Swedish news-stands—and it's obvious someone has done his or her homework.

cars that don't show obvious rust probably don't have any. These Volvos develop rust problems in all the typical locations, and it's not unusual to see holes dotting the joint between fenders and body. It's a good idea, of course, to closely examine these cars for rust because rust repair can be expensive and with unit-body construction, there's only sheet metal between you and the road.

Restored cars are actually more of a problem in this regard. Make sure that there's more metal than plastic in the body

1963 PV544	
Dimensions	
Wheelbase	102.5in
Track	51.0/51.7in
Length	175in
Width	62.5in
Height	61.5in
Weight	2,160lb
Engine	
Type	Ohv I-4
Bore & stroke	3.31x3.15in (84x80mm)
Displacement	108.5ci (1778cc)
Compression	8.5:1
Fuel delivery	Two SU (1V)
Horsepower	90bhp @ 5000rpm
Torque	105lb-ft @ 3500rpm
Chassis and Drivetrain	
Layout, engine/drivetrain	F/R
Frame/body	Unit steel
Transmission	Four-speed manual
Rear axle ratio	4.10:1
Suspension, F/R	A-arm/live axle
Tires	5.90x15in
Brakes	Drum/drum
Performance	
0-60mph	14.1sec
1/4 mile	19.1sec @ 70mph
Fuel mileage	25–29mpg
Top speed	92mph

It *looks* like a PV544, but deep down it's a separate frame instead of the unit-body construction of the sedan. Originally designated the PV445, it was nicknamed the Duett, for "two cars in one." It was produced in station wagon form, or in panel van or pickup truck configuration. A few convertible 544s were made on the 445 frame as well. In 1960 the designation was changed to 210 with changes to the frame. Though the production of the bare chassis stopped in 1962, the Duett/210 stayed in production until 1967. This 1967 has an accessory roof rack and aftermarket "gangster shade" popular at the time. The B18 in this Duett was replaced with a B20 by owner Chris Buscher.

(take along a magnet). Fortunately, rust repair panels are available for many of the common rust locations. Rear bumpers, however, are very difficult to find.

Don't be upset if a late 444 has a 544 grille or taillights. A lot of them came from the factory with the "wrong" equipment on them. As one 444 owner comments, "Whatever Sven and Lars put on it." Different outside rearview mirrors were also used in no particular pattern.

The good news is that the engines are durable and hard to break, the cars are still reasonably priced, and they're fun to drive and attract a lot of attention. You probably won't get rich off the appreciation—there's not enough sex appeal in the Volvo that looks like an old Ford—but the 444/544 certainly isn't going to get any cheaper. One observer calls the 444/544 "really a sleeper."

An expert suggests watching Duetts, which can be worth more than the sedans if only because of their relative scarcity in the United States. Either way, your return on investment should be good with these first official immigrant Volvos.

P1900 1956-1957

Volvo's First Sports Car

It left as quickly as it had come, leaving hardly a ripple to mark its passing. Yet for an exotic Volvo, one would be hard pressed to find a better example than the P1900.

The short story of the P1900 began in 1953 when Assar Gabrielsson made one of his periodic visits to the United States. He observed the booming interest in sports cars in the country, not only the imported MGs and so forth, but also the Italo-American Nash-Healey and the wholly domestic Chevrolet Corvette. The latter with its fiberglass body must have been particularly intriguing, for Gabrielsson included in his itinerary the California fiberglass firm Glasspar, which was making boats and car bodies, such as the

The Volvo P1900 combined the B14 engine with a special chassis and a fiberglass body designed by Glasspar, an American kit-car manufacturer. Owners are David and Deborah Woods.

Woodill Wildfire. With importation of the PV444 pending, what better way of attracting American attention than a sports car?

Glasspar had a design in Gabrielsson's hands before he left for home, and he forwarded it to Sweden with instructions to develop a suitable chassis immediately. Glasspar had prototype bodies arriving in Göteborg not much later, although none of them would be used, Volvo intending to use its own.

The frame developed—the PV444 unit-body not amenable to use, and the PV445 not appropriate—was of steel tubes and rugged side-members, with independent front suspension and a live axle on coil springs at the rear. The engine was the B14A with twin SU carburetors and rated at 70bhp at 5500rpm. Although a ZF five-speed manual transmission had been considered, the in-house three-speed manual, complete with a shifter that seemingly could double as a meter stick, was used.

Several modifications to the Glasspar design were made in Sweden, though its racy open-mouthed grille and headlights well integrated into the fender line remained. It was an attractive automobile, especially for the era, one that today remains handsome if not up to date.

The car made its public showing at Torslanda Airport near Göteborg on June 2, 1954, and its auto show debut at Brussels in January 1955. Testing then took place in Sweden during 1955, where a number of defects were found and corrected. Deliveries to customers actually didn't begin until the spring of 1956, sales being made in Sweden as well as abroad. Demand, however, proved low.

A mere forty-four cars were made in 1956 and only twenty-three in 1957, with most of the latter year's cars bound for the United States. A total of twenty-seven are believed to have been sent to America in all. Most of the thirty-eight cars sold in Sweden are said still to be in existence, though only a handful survive in the United States, fewer still restored.

What killed the P1900, in addition to low sales, was the opinion of Gunnar Engellau, who had taken over as chief at Volvo in 1956,

1955 P1900	
Dimensions	
Wheelbase	94.5in
Track	N/A
Length	N/A
Width	N/A
Height	N/A
Weight	1,900lb
Engine	
Type	Ohv I-4
Bore & stroke	2.95x3.15in (75x80mm)
Displacement	86.3ci (1414cc)
Compression	7.8:1
Fuel delivery	Two SU (1V)
Horsepower	70bhp @ 6000rpm
Torque	76lb-ft @ 3500rpm
Chassis and Drivetrain	
Layout, engine/drivetrain	F/R
Frame/body	Steel tube/fiberglass
Transmissions	Three-speed manual
Rear axle ratio	N/A (approx. 4:55:1)
Suspension, F/R	A-arms/live axle
Tires	5.90x15in
Brakes	Drum/drum
Performance	
0-60mph	N/A
1/4 mile	N/A
Fuel mileage	N/A
Top speed	96mph

Rear end of the P1900 has a hatch-lid for the trunk and generic taillights.

Dash is complete and sports car-like. The steering wheel is straight from the sedan.

that the car was not up to Volvo standards. Furthermore, it was expensive to produce and didn't fit into Volvo's product line. Engellau pulled the plug. Those few cars that remain are rolling might-have-beens. Even still, the P1900 was Europe's first fiberglass car and the inspiration for the P1800.

What to Look For

Good hunting. There are only a handful of these Nordic nightingales known to be in the United States, and only a couple of them are in good condition. Those in Europe are likely to carry high prices. On the other hand, you may discover one festering in a barn somewhere—it still happens—and the car's scarcity makes restoration of even a find in poor condition not only worthwhile but morally imperative. Of course, it won't be cheap, and finding parts for the B14 engine won't be any easier for the P1900 than for the PV444. But if scarcity is any measure, this is the king of postwar Volvos—which is ironic because from a practical standpoint, it was Volvo's worst car. It's best, however, not to question these things.

Rear view of the P1900 shows a well-balanced if somewhat bland design.

Convertible top for P1900 was simple and well proportioned. *Volvo*

Chapter 4

120 Series 1956-1970

The Eleven-Year Car

Volvo called it the Amazon—from Greek mythology, a female warrior—and prepared public relations photos of the car with a toga-clad, sword-wielding model alongside. The concept was rather preposterous, to say the least, and when after two years on the market in Europe it came to the United States in April 1959, it was known simply as the 122S.

It wasn't because reason had prevailed, however. The fact was that Kreidler, a (then) West German motorcycle manufacturer, held the rights to Amazon (an interesting concept in itself), and after negotiations allowed the name to be used on domestic models only. The series numbers that were used instead apparently came from the car's development project, which was 1200 (the PV444 had been 1100, but there's no law that logic has anything to do with it). The base model was known as the 120, and the sport model, with dual carbs and a four-speed, was the 122S, which was the only version exported to the United States.

The early home market 122 had Amazon fender script, replaced by a 121 badge on two doors.

1959 122S	
Dimensions	
Wheelbase	102.4in
Track	51.7/51.7in
Length	173in
Width	63.5in
Height	59.2in
Weight	2,390lb
Engine	
Type	Ohv I-4
Bore & stroke	3.125x3.15in (79.4x80.0mm)
Displacement	96.6ci (1586cc)
Compression	8.2:1
Fuel delivery	Two SU (1V)
Horsepower	85bhp @ 5500rpm
Torque	87lb-ft @ 3500rpm
Chassis and Drivetrain	
Layout, engine/drivetrain	F/R
Frame/body	Unit steel
Transmission	Four-speed manual
Rear axle ratio	4.55:1
Suspension, F/R	A-arms/live axle
Tires	5.90x15in
Brakes	Drum/drum
Performance	
0-60mph	16.2sec
¼ mile	20.0sec @ 66mph
Fuel mileage	24–27mpg
Top speed	91.9mph

But that's getting ahead of the story. The new 120, which debuted in Sweden on September 1, 1956, and went on sale there in 1957, was stylistically a giant step into the future from the PV444, though overall the 120 still had the look of America's yesterday today. *Road & Track* even felt compelled to note that it was not, as some suggested, made using 1953 Willys sedan dies!

In some ways, the car was mechanically similar to the PV444. The engine, the 1583cc B16A, was basically the PV444's four-cylinder with a bore job, and would be shared with the PV444 as well. But the chassis was new and the suspension different, the front suspension arms now unequal-length and ball joints replacing king pins. The rear suspension, although still a live axle on coil springs, received a revised system of locating arms.

Even though on an identical 102.5in wheelbase and similar track, the 120 had more interior room than the PV444 and was a true five-seater. The PV544 was classified as a five-passenger car, but it was just barely wide

American-spec 122S, complete with bumper guard and New Jersey license plates. Note the heavily chromed grille with the big cross bar. *Volvo photo; Automobile Quarterly archives*

enough in the rear. A long truck-like shift lever angling back from under the dash was still there, however. The parking brake was moved from under the dash to the floor to the left of the driver's seat (instead of between the seats so that if the car were ever to be equipped with a bench seat it wouldn't have to be moved).

From a corporate culture standpoint, it's significant to note that the Volvo circle-and-arrow logo was removed from the grille, which was a stylish double opening, trimmed in chrome with a heavy chromed horizontal bar backed by meshwork. The Volvo diagonal was gone. The logo had not completely disappeared; it was merely exiled to the trunk lid handle.

The 122S, as imported to America (and sold in Sweden as the Amazon Sport—another interesting concept), produced 85bhp and was equipped with the old-style Volvo four-speed. The new Volvo four-speed was the big mechanical refinement for the 122S in 1960, the PV544 getting this transmission as well.

1960-1964 and the B18

The B18B engine arrived in 1961. This 1778cc overhead-valve four-cylinder bore

While American market 122s came with red rear brake and turn lenses, European market cars had turn signals in amber.

only superficial resemblance to its predecessor. Introduced first on the sporty P1800, the new engine had five main bearings with caps that not only bolted on but keyed into the block. The bearing surfaces themselves were compared favorably to the Chevrolet small-block V-8. It was so stout that it had run

120 Series Production

Model	Series	Production Dates	Number Built
P120 4dr	A	1956-1958	5,184
	B	1958-1960	49,214
	D	1960-1961	29,900
	E	1961-1962	28,500
	F	1962-1963	27,200
	G	1963-1964	26,400
	K	1964-1965	27,400
	L	1965-1966	31,250
	M	1966-1967	9,160
			Total: 234,209
P130 2dr	A	1961-1962	10,500
	B	1962-1963	29,500
	D	1963-1964	44,600
	E	1964-1965	59,800
	F	1965-1966	72,550

Model	Series	Production Dates	Number Built
	M	1966-1967	62,950
	P	1967-1968	32,600
	S	1968-1969	27,500
	T	1969-1970	19,918
			Total: 359,917
P220 SW	A	1962	1,400
	B	1962-1963	6,875
	D	1963-1964	9,675
	E	1964-1965	11,450
	F	1965-1966	15,200
	M	1966-1967	17,200
	P	1967-1968	8,500
	S	1968-1969	2,897
			Total: 73,196

at maximum rpm—5500—for 500 straight hours on the dynamometer with no ill effect.

An unusual split cooling system had coolant circulated directly to the head by the water pump, the coolant thereupon returning to the radiator. The engine block itself relied on thermosiphon for cooling.

The B18B (Sport) version produced 90hp, fifteen more than the B18A standard domestic version, thanks to the former's dual SU carburetors and other changes. Actual ratings for the B18B were 90bhp at 5000rpm and 105lb-ft of torque at 4000rpm. Last but not least, a B-18 badge was mounted on the left-side grille opening, about as far as one went in status climbing in a Volvo.

Also in 1961 came a two-door sedan version of the 120 Series, followed in 1962 by an Estate, or four-door station wagon, version. *Road & Track* tested a 122S B18 and recorded a time of 14.5 seconds for 0–60mph, and 19.5 seconds for the standing-start quarter mile. A three-speed Borg-Warner automatic transmission was optional in 1963 on the four-door sedan, but *Road & Track* noted that the automatic added a couple of seconds to the 0–60mph times and took "part of the fun and pleasure" from the 122S.

1965-1966

Front disc and rear drum brakes went on all 120s in 1965. That model year also saw a

Second-series grille is shown on a 1966 122S two-door. A single stamping replaced the more complex grille of the first series in 1965. Owner is David Humphreys.

The ornate trunk handle on the original design yielded to a handle of more subtlety on later models.

The final grille design was this doubled bar on the 122S wagon of Robert and Edith Newman.

An accessory wood-rimmed steering wheel graces interior of this 1966 122S two-door. Owner is Jerry Sira.

new grille, a one-piece stamping per side imitating the earlier design with a major horizontal bar and smaller horizontal and vertical bars.

Other changes included ventilated (rather than solid) wheel discs, heating ducts to the rear seat area, and a dash-mounted grab handle for the front-seat passenger. Galvanized sill sections made 1965 and later

The tailgate on the 122S wagon opened in clamshell fashion. Owner is Michael Hamilton.

Volvos were assembled from ckd (completely knocked down) kits in Halifax, Nova Scotia; some of them had Volvo Canadian badges, as does this 1966 122S of David Humphreys.

1965 122S Automatic	
Dimensions	
Wheelbase	102.5in
Track	51.7/51.7in
Length	175in
Width	63.75in
Height	59.25in
Weight	2,570lb
Engine	
Type	Ohv I-4
Bore & stroke	3.31x3.15in (84.0x80.0mm)
Displacement	109ci (1780cc)
Compression	8.5:1
Fuel delivery	Two SU (1V)
Horsepower	90bhp @ 5000rpm
Torque	105lb-ft @ 3500rpm
Chassis and Drivetrain	
Layout, engine/drivetrain	F/R
Frame/body	Unit steel
Transmission	Three-speed automatic
Rear axle ratio	4.10:1
Suspension, F/R	A-arm/live axle
Tires	6.00x15in
Brakes	Disc/drum
Performance	
0-60mph	15.8sec
1/4 mile	20.6sec @ 67mph
Fuel mileage	20–23mpg
Top speed	90mph

Big moose-spotting driving lights are common on cars in rural areas of Sweden, but this 122, identified as a 1965 or 1966 by its grille, is a neatly modified and well-kept driver.

120s more rust resistant. The radiator blind, controlled by a chain pull from the driver's seat, was eliminated; Volvo apparently considered it superfluous.

A new Volvo tradition began in 1965—and it was a well-advertised one at that: the installation of orthopedically correct seats with variable lumbar support, though a screwdriver was required to make any changes. The seat bottom angle could also be changed and the seatbacks reclined. To top it off, the seats were upholstered in a new textile-reinforced perforated vinyl.

1967

In 1967 the new Volvo 144 was introduced and the 120 Series updated with a rear

The dashboard on the 1967 122S could almost be American with its horizontal speedometer and the flashy horn ring on the steering wheel. But note the long shift lever. Owner is Michael Hamilton.

The 122S design adapted well to a station wagon version. The 1967 wagon of Robert and Edith Newman wears a Volvo accessory roof rack.

An aftermarket air conditioning compressor and valve cover has been fitted to this 122S. Fuel line runs to the intake manifold to pre-warm the fuel: this is emissions control circa 1967. Owner is Michael Hamilton.

Well-kept 122s like this 1967 to 1970 can still be seen in daily use in Sweden.

Rare 123GT can be identified by fender-mounted mirrors and the huge driving lights, as well as fender badge. The 123GT did not have the B20 engine as per the owner-added badge on the grille. Owner is Jerry Sira.

The 123GT was a factory high-performance special with mud flaps—but then, it's a Volvo. *Volvo*

suspension from the new model, having longer trailing arms to keep both wheels on the ground during severe cornering. A twin-branch exhaust manifold, sealed cooling system, modified clutch, and an alternator in-stead of the generator were also among upgrades that included redesigned three-point front seatbelts and the addition of mounting points for rear belts.

As on the 1800S, a new grille texture with doubled bars went on all 120 Series cars. Performance of US (and domestic Sport) models was improved by an additional 10hp from the engine, now up to 100bhp.

123GT

For even more power there was the 123GT, which came with the high-output engine of the 1800S, good for 115bhp at 6000rpm. The 123GT also got the same gear-box ratios as the 1800S, firmer shocks, and radial tires as standard equipment. There was a 7000rpm Smith's tachometer mounted on top of the dash as well.

More visible indicators to set the 123GT apart included twin fender mirrors, giant fog

In Trollhattan, home of Saab automobiles, this Volvo displays divided loyalty by wearing *Saab wheels.*

Darth Vader meets 1967 122S: Black 122S had iPd suspension and air dam, 14x7in wheels, and a 160hp, 2133cc engine under the hood. Owner is Robert Gordon. *iPd*

and driving lights—one each—on the front bumper, and chrome trim rings for the wheels. And of course, there was a special fender badge.

The 123GT was in fact homologated with the Federation Internationale de l'Automobile (FIA) for rallying; however, Volvo did not actually produce the 5,000 cars required. Only about 1,500 were made, half in 1967, half in 1968.

1968: The 122S Eclipsed

The 122S stayed in Volvo's US sales line-up in 1968, but the star was clearly the 144S, and the 122 was withdrawn from the American marketplace for the 1969 model year.

For the home-market 120 (still called the Amazon), Volvo installed the B20A (90bhp) and B20B (118bhp) beginning in August 1968, and only the two-door sedan was available. The last 120 was built on July 3, 1969.

A total of 234,209 four-door (P120), 359,917 two door (P130), and 73,196 station wagons (P220) had been built, of which 60 percent were exported.

What to Look For

It seems no matter whom you ask, nobody has anything bad to say about the 120 Series. They're sturdy and everything is available and/or repairable. Some enthusiasts prefer 1967 and later due to the improved rear suspension.

Watch for rust in all the usual locations, plus look under the car where the reinforce-

ments from the front end come under the floor pan. Rust in this area can seriously weaken the car and threaten its structural integrity.

Dashboard covers are no longer available from the dealers, but a good upholsterer can refit the dash if necessary. Otherwise, things like gauges, switches, fenders, and trim are available, and wiper motors rebuildable. Window mechanisms sometimes drop the windows in the tracks, but are easily fixed after the inner door panel is removed.

Rubber donuts on the rear suspension links tend to wear out, resulting in axle windup and rear-end noise. The parts are easy to get, although it's a nuisance. A polyurethane donut kit is available from iPd Company, Incorporated, and will be longer lasting than the original rubber pieces.

Parts may become harder to get over the next five years as the B18 engine gets older. It may not be time to hoard yet, but it will be more expensive for those who delay purchase.

Likewise, prices for whole cars will only climb. The hot rod of the 120 set is the 123GT and, rare as it is, will demand a higher price. Because there weren't many made, it will be hard to find. On the other hand, since it's fairly obscure to all but 120 enthusiasts, it may not carry any premium if you are lucky enough to find one on a generic used car lot somewhere.

The station wagons, for some reason, also seem to bring a higher price.

★ ★ ★ ★ ★	**P1800**
★ ★ ★ ★ ★	**1800S**
★ ★ ★ ★ ★	**1800E**
★ ★ ★ ★	**1800ES**

1800 Series 1961-1973

The Sexy Swedes

It may have been a Swedish car but, at least in the beginning, the P1800 came from all over. The prototypes had been built in Italy, the body panels were stamped and assembled by the Pressed Steel Company Limited in Scotland, while Jensen Motors from near Birmingham, England, completed assembly and painted them. The instruments were all Smiths and most of the electrics and the original-equipment battery were by Lucas, both British, as are the SU carburetors, Girling brakes, and Laycock de Normanville overdrive. The ZF steering gear was German, as well as the SWF windshield washer pump and the Bosch ignition and spark plugs. The fuel pump and air cleaners were from AC, an

The original P1800 had these unusual bull-horn bumpers, complex egg-crate grille, and full wheel covers.

American company, and the wiper motors were Autolite. The Spicer rear axle and Delco shocks also were of US origin, the Pirelli tires from Italy. Well, at least the powertrain was all Swedish. . . .

Yet due to a lack of capacity at Volvo facilities and foreign accessories—Sweden didn't have much of a support industry—the foreign assembly didn't change the basic nature of the automobile. This clearly was a Volvo. The B18B engine was completely new and at 100bhp the hottest ever from Volvo, but as a pushrod design that borrowed heavily from its predecessors it was hardly leading edge. *Road & Track* stated the car was "designed for tractability, rather than racing." Faint praise indeed for a *sports* car.

Still there was that styling, about which *Car and Driver* noted, "From its attractive egg-crate grille to its kicked-up rear fenders, it looks trim and fast. . . ." And inside, *Road & Track* called it "done in the rather futuristic fashion that characterizes the U.S.-built car." Not the sturdy simplicity of the PV544 or P122S. Fortunately, the shift lever for the four-speed transmission was relocated rearward

and shortened, a more car-like arrangement than the sedans.

Like its more pedestrian siblings, the P1800 had unequal-length A-arm front suspension, with a live axle on coil springs at the rear. *Car and Driver* found an unrelenting understeer when pressed, to the point of lifting (and spinning) the inside rear wheel. But then, the magazine notes, "Throughout the rest of the cornering spectrum, the P1800 is a pure delight."

Unlike the sedans, with their American-style horizontal-band speedometers, the P1800 had a round speedometer, calibrated to 120mph though in 20mph lumps. Between the speedo and the 7000rpm tach were vertical-bar coolant and oil temperature gauges; round dial gauges for fuel level and oil pressure and a clock were centered over the transmission hump.

The P1800 was introduced at the Brussels International Motor Show in January 1960, although it didn't go into production until May 1961, reaching the United States that year as well. The first 6,000 cars were assembled in England, with assembly switching to Sweden during the spring of 1963 for the next 2,000 cars, called the B Series.

1963-1966

The original 100hp engine was upgraded for the D Series, having skipped the C Series, commencing in August 1963. The new model, now called the 1800S, had more comfortable front seats and the rear seat, never

1961 P1800	
Dimensions	
Wheelbase	96.5in
Track	52/52in
Length	173in
Width	67in
Height	51in
Weight	2,500lb
Engine	
Type	Ohv I-4
Bore & stroke	3.31x3.15in (84.0x80.0mm)
Displacement	108.5ci (1780cc)
Compression	9.5:1
Fuel delivery	Two SU (1V)
Horsepower	100bhp @ 5500rpm
Torque	108lb-ft @ 4000rpm
Chassis and Drivetrain	
Layout, engine/drivetrain	F/R
Frame/body	Unit steel
Transmission	Four-speed manual plus overdrive
Rear axle ratio	4.56:1
Suspension, F/R	A-arm/live axle
Tires	5.90x15in
Brakes	Disc/drum
Performance	
0-60mph	12.4sec
1/4 mile	18.0sec @ 72mph
Fuel mileage	22–26mpg
Top speed	105mph

Grille of P1800 not only looked like an egg crate, but slotted together like one as well.

usable by anything larger than small children or pets, could be folded down for additional storage space. A small storage space below the rear window was eliminated, however, and the Volvo badge and flag emblem was removed from the C-pillar. A usable eight more horsepower were found, however, which made it worthwhile.

The E Series began production in August 1964, and was easily recognized by the

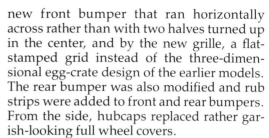

new front bumper that ran horizontally across rather than with two halves turned up in the center, and by the new grille, a flat-stamped grid instead of the three-dimensional egg-crate design of the earlier models. The rear bumper was also modified and rub strips were added to front and rear bumpers. From the side, hubcaps replaced rather garish-looking full wheel covers.

Production of the F Series began in August 1965, headlined by a second power increase, this time to 115bhp thanks primarily to a new exhaust manifold.

Volvo skipped letters in the alphabet to the M Series in August 1966. The most notable changes were yet another grille (doubled the horizontal bars, like its sedan siblings) and straightening the chrome trim, which had previously followed the character line in the door panel.

A tuning kit was also made available for US buyers who desired more power including:
- High compression (11.0:1) cylinder head with larger valves
- High-lift camshaft
- Lighter flywheel
- Oil pump and timing gear covers

Closer look at the early character line and doorhandle, free standing on the P1800.

Only the P1800 had this Volvo badge with yellow and blue flag stripes on the C-pillar.

The grille was changed to a cheaper and less-attractive stamping for the E and F Series 1800S.

Personalized with aftermarket wheels, this P1800 restored by Sue and Scott Hart (Sue overhauled the engine) shows how the original side trim followed the character line. *iPd*

The P1800 had Volvo spelled out in individual letters across its rear and a fuel filter on top of the left rear flank, through which water often found its way to the fuel tank to cause rust. Note that the taillight lenses should be all red, but only bi-color lenses are now readily available.

The 1968 M Series 1800S received a new double-bar grille, here with Washington Volvo Club and Volvo mileage badge attached.

A constant theme in 1800 Series advertising was getting a Ferrari or Aston Martin at a Volvo price—a theme later repeated with its comparison of a Lamborghini Countach with a trailer to a Volvo Turbo wagon.

- Pulley hub
- Carburetor needles, richer than standard
- Lighter springs for carburetor damper pistons
- Special Bosch plugs (W280 T 13 S) and coil (TK 12 A10)
- Tuned header

The kit raised horsepower to 135bhp without a loss of flexibility at a cost of $299 (and about $100 more for installation), this on a car that listed for $4,200 in 1966.

1967-1969

Volvo skipped again, this time to the P Series, in August 1967. The new US safety regulations ushered in a collapsible steering column for all markets and for the United States, front seat headrests, and safety knobs on the dash. Other changes included a new three-spoked steering wheel and a repositioned choke knob.

Installation of the bored-out B20B engine began with the S Series in the fall of 1968, although the 2.0 liter engine didn't inspire a name change. It also didn't produce a significantly higher peak horsepower rating, only 118bhp thanks to a lower 9.5:1 compression ratio. Torque increased from 112lb-ft at 4000rpm to 123lb-ft at 3500, providing more

The P1800 and 1800S had direct-reading (via capillary tubes) oil- and coolant-temperature gauges between the speedometer and tachometer.

The change from P1800 to 1800S was accompanied by changes to the side trim, which now incorporated the doorhandle.

Volvoville, a Long Island, New York, based dealer converted coupes to convertibles and ran single-column-wide ads in national magazines.

Imagine admitting your car is heavy. Volvo did so with a twist in this 1969 ad.

flexibility and easier driving. For the United States, Zenith-Stromberg carburetors replaced the SU carbs, which remained on the domestic models.

Other changes in the B20B engine included a cooling fan clutch that limited fan speed to about 3000rpm, reducing noise, and quieter air cleaners that reduced noise from the carburetors. Gone was the oil-to-water oil cooler, deemed no longer necessary because of a higher-capacity oil pump and better oil. Changes to the clutch and final-drive ratio completed what was externally visible only by the B-20 badge on the grille.

1800E

The carbureted 2.0 liter engine lasted less than one year before the T Series and the introduction of Bosch Jetronic fuel injection. The new model would be popularly known as the 1800E (for *Einspritz*, "injection" in German, or "electronic fuel injection" in English) and would wear an 1800E badge on the rear.

The 1800E could also be identified by the matte-black grille, black exhaust vents from the interior on the rear fenders, and wider,

The 1970 1800E got a new blacked-out grille.

The 1971 1800E had a new nose badget with rounded bottom with crown on top but the same grille as 1970.

The grille on the E Series (starting 8/1964) was a simple stamping that was cheaper and looked it. A new straight front bumper started with the E Series too.

European-specification car wore alloy wheels standard on the 1970-1971 1800E only. *Volvo*

cast-aluminum wheels. Inside, a new dash, with white-on-black instruments on a flat-black background, replaced the earlier design that prompted complaints of unreadability. Alas, wood from the bogus tree adorned the dashboard itself.

The spritzer engine got a horsepower boost. With a 10.5:1 compression ratio, larger

The 1972 1800E had a vertical-slat plastic grille and rectangular badge.

1970 1800E	
Dimensions	
Wheelbase	96.5in
Track	51.6/51.6in
Length	171.3in
Width	66.9in
Height	50.4in
Weight	2,535lb
Engine	
Type	Ohv I-4
Bore & stroke	3.50x3.15in. (89x80mm)
Displacement	121ci (1986cc)
Compression	10.5:1
Fuel delivery	Bosch K-Jetronic injection
Horsepower	130bhp @ 6000rpm
Torque	130lb-ft @ 3500rpm
Chassis and Drivetrain	
Layout, engine/drivetrain	F/R
Frame/body	Unit steel
Transmission	Four-speed manual plus overdrive
Rear axle ratio	4.30:1
Suspension, F/R	A-arm/live axle
Tires	165x15in
Brakes	Disc/disc
Performance	
0-60mph	10.1sec
1/4 mile	17.5sec @ 80mph
Fuel mileage	20.9mpg
Top speed	115mph

By 1972, the Volvo script on the rear of the 1800 had shrunk but was joined by a model designation badge. The fuel filler was moved to the side of the rear fender beginning with the 1970 model year.

The only year for the black plastic grille and rectangular hood badge on the coupe was 1972.

The 1972 model year was the last for the coupe version of the 1800E.

44

intake valves and a new, better-breathing camshaft, the 2.0 liter engine produced 130bhp at 6000rpm. A new four-speed-plus-overdrive gearbox from ZF and four-wheel disc brakes were other distinguishing features of the 1800E.

The U Series 1800E went into production in August 1970, for the first time with an optional automatic transmission (the Borg-Warner BW35 three-speed with the selector mounted on the driveshaft tunnel). The Volvo four-speed transmission, strengthened to handle the torque of the B20, replaced the ZF substituted the year before.

While the W Series 1800E coupe went into production in August 1971, it was to be the last time around, with production ending June 22, 1972. The grille, now black ABS

Hinges and locks attached directly to the all-glass hatch of the 1800ES. The big glass tailgate, however, gave everyone a look at what was in your trunk.

The 1800ES breathed new life into Volvo's sports car line, and some consider it better looking than the coupe. It was, regardless, the world's only sports wagon. This 1800ES has been fitted with aftermarket wheels. *iPd*

Rare and special 1972 Volvo accessory wheels.

1972 1800ES	
Dimensions	
Wheelbase	96.5in
Track	51.6/51.6in
Length	172.6in
Width	66.9in
Height	50.4in
Weight	2,570lb
Engine	
Type	Ohv I-4
Bore & stroke	3.50x3.15in (89x80mm)
Displacement	121ci (1986cc)
Compression	8.7:1
Fuel delivery	Bosch K-Jetronic injection
Horsepower	112bhp @ 6000rpm
Torque	115lb-ft @ 3500rpm
Chassis and Drivetrain	
Layout, engine/drivetrain	F/R
Frame/body	Unit steel
Transmission	Four-speed manual plus overdrive
Rear axle ratio	4.30:1
Suspension, F/R	A-arm/live axle
Tires	185/70HR-15
Brakes	Disc/disc
Performance	
0-60mph	11.3sec
1/4 mile	18.2sec @ 74mph
Fuel mileage	22.5mpg
Top speed	116mph

Grille and side molding identifies this car as third-generation 1800. Wheels are aftermarket.

plastic, had vertical bars and the hood emblem was changed to rectangular. Wheel design was changed and a tint was applied to the windows. Another 5hp were found for the home-market engine, but US emission engines (the B20F) lost five horses.

1800ES

But the demise of the coupe wasn't the end of the line that began with the P1800. The W Series 1800ES started production at the same time as the 1800E coupe. The 1800ES was, as *Car and Driver* called it, a "sportwagon," and Volvo called it a sports car that "not only hauls, it carries." Definitely not a coupe, it wasn't a station wagon either ("there isn't even enough room in the back . . . for two consenting adults," said *Car and Driver*). But it got a couple more years out of a shape dated after eleven years of production and provided a unique vehicle, a sports car that could carry stuff.

The W Series 1800ES was trimmed just like its coupe counterpart, except that the

In its final year, the 1800ES suffered the indignity of a crash bumper, which projected farther from the body than on earlier models. *Volvo*

47

1800 Series Production and Serial Numbers

Model	Series	Production Dates	Serial Numbers	Number Built
P1800	A	5/1961-3/1963	0001-6000	6,000
1800S	B	4/1963-7/1963	6001-8000	2,000
	D	8/1963-7/1964	8001-12499	4,500
	E	8/1964-7/1965	12500-16499	4,000
	F	8/1965-7/1966	16500-20999	4,500
	M	8/1966-7/1967	21000-25499	4,500
	P	8/1967-7/1968	25500-28299	2,800
	S	8/1968-7/1969	28300-30000	1,693
1800E	T	8/1969-7/1970	30001-32799	2,799
	U	8/1970-7/1971	32800-37549	4,750
	W	8/1971-6/1972	37550-39414	1,865
				Total: 39,385
1800ES	W	8/1971-7/1972	1-3069	3,070
	Y	8/1972-6/1973*	3070-8077	5,007
				Total: 8,077

*Volvo 1800ES number 8,077 left the factory at 2pm on June 27, 1973.

"flatback" had a large, unframed glass door, to which the hinges and latch attached directly.

The Y Series was comprised of the 1800ES only. This final iteration was marred by US safety and emission requrements—impact-absorbing bumpers disrupted the lines of the car and the US-spec B20F engine was reduced to 112bhp on a lead-free diet. Other modifications included side-door guard beams, modified windshield wipers, a new first-gear ratio, and all fire-resistant materials in the interior. A total of 8,077 ES models were produced.

An 1800 convertible was produced by Volvoville, an Amityville, New York, dealership. Some thirty to maybe as many as fifty were made by shops contracted to Volvoville, starting in about 1965. Thanks to the cabin design of the 1800, the result is clean and looks like it could have been planned as a convertible from the beginning. The top was a rather primitive device in the British tradition of a frame, with fitted fabric that snapped over the top.

A total of 47,462 1800s were produced in twelve years, most going to the United States. For example, in the last three years, the United States received 79 percent of those made.

What to Look For

The 1800 Series is the most desirable of the large-production Volvos. The early cars made by Jensen have some extra cachet among collectors, whether for the bull-horn bumpers, or because they were different, who knows?

Then, too, the ES of 1972 and 1973, with the "shooting brake" body, is more valuable to some enthusiasts. The wagon-like style does add practicality—the 1800s, like most sports cars, don't have excessive trunk room—but collectors probably care less about that than their more limited production numbers. Overall, the prospect is good for value to increase. Auctioneer Rick Cole put the Volvo 1800 on his Gold List in 1991.

Rust is your enemy on the 1800. Some owners have found leaking problems, even with new seals, and cars left out in the elements can suffer from severe rusting problems. Seals are available, though replacing all the trunk, door, and other seals can be expensive. The Jensen-built cars were notorious for leaky seams and as a result, finding an early 1800 that isn't rust damaged is unusual.

The 1800 can also suffer from rusty gas tank syndrome: the drain line for the area behind the fuel filler door gets clogged, the area fills with water, and the water then leaks into the tank past a hardened and cracked filler cap seal. The final result is a rusty gas tank. Lift the mat over the tank and look for blisters.

Rust also attacks the floor and undercarriage. Look first at the jacking point under the front edge of the door, then the cross-member support. The rocker panel has two seams under either end of the door that were leaded in at the factory. These will be putty if repair work has been done. Extreme cases of rust will rot the floor pans away, so aways look under the floor mat. Rust is also common around the headlamps and parking lamps. Patch panels are available, but better to start with a solid car.

Duane Matejka, 1800 specialist, claims that 1800s are not more susceptible to rust than other marques, but appear to be so because they keep running when any other car would have been scrapped. Nevertheless, he advises prospective buyers to look for rust for that very reason.

The headlamp buckets, incidentally, are interchangeable with many British cars that used Lucas parts. If you can't find a Volvo part, an MG part may do. Volvo used all-red taillamps until the ES, when red and amber lenses were introduced. Now only the bicolor lenses are available, and serious collectors will pay more than twice their price for the correct all-red ones.

The 1800s have the same suspension as the 120 Series, so look for worn donuts in the suspension links. As on the 120s, these are replaceable.

On 1968 cars (and late 1967), the first year with dual-circuit braking systems, brake master cylinders were made by Wagner. These master cylinders are no longer available, but kits to adapt later ATE master cylinders are available. Better yet, the master cylinders can be honed and sleeved, maintaining the car's originality.

Cynics say the gauges on the early cars never work, especially the oil and water temperature gauges between the tach and speedo. These gauges are direct reading from heat-conducting capillary tubes that are sensitive to damage from ham-handed mechanics. Fortunately, repair parts are available.

The 1800E and 1800ES cars equipped with the Bosch D-Jetronic fuel injection run better than their carbureted predecessors, but wiring becomes brittle with age and can break or short, especially where it passes behind the head and is exposed to heat. Replacement looms are no longer available (they were expensive anyway), so to repair one you must either shop the salvage yards or replace the individual wire. The latter is complicated, by the way: the wires are tagged on each end but are identical for the rest of their lengths. The system's sensors and rubber boots for the connectors are still available from Volvo. These cars can also be aggravated by maddening electrical gremlins.

The 1970 1800 did not have a "thermal timer" on its fuel-injection system; enrichment occurred only when the engine was cranking. Otherwise, there was no choke effect. Another anomaly of the 1970 system was injector shutoff on closed throttle; the fuel-injection system would provide no fuel until rpm dropped to about 1200. It feels odd, but there's no adverse effect.

★★	142S, 144S, 145S, 142E,
	144E, 145E, (1971-1974)
★★¹/₂	164, 164E
★★★	142E (1971)

140 and 160 Series 1966-1975

The First Modern Volvos

When *Road & Track* first viewed the Volvo 144, the magazine said it was "pretty much what we expected—a slightly larger sedan with a contemporary, but not radical, body and refinements to the various mechanical systems . . . a logical development of a logical car." *Car and Driver* was about as succinct: "It was roomier, more comfortable, and it had a number of new features that were extremely worthwhile, but it just didn't have that certain hard-to-define pizzazz." Faint praise for a new model, sort of like saying Mr. Spock is not much fun at a party but at least he doesn't spill the dip on the carpet.

First-series 142S has stamped grille. Note that the 142S Volvo guy still wears a suit (like the 122S Volvo guy), but has lost his fedora. *Volvo photo;* Automobile Quarterly *archives*

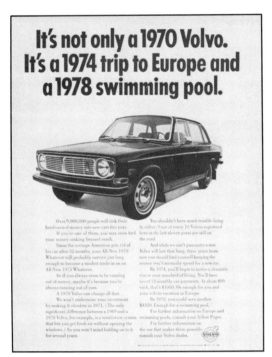

Volvo turned a 144 on its head for this 1969 ad, which, copy aside, gives a good view of a Volvo's underworkings.

Volvo also advertised the 144 right side up.

That is hardly fair. The appeal of a Volvo has always been deeper than fads and trendy sheet metal, which is good because the relatively small Swedish company has never been able to afford either. The 144 was, in fact, both a continuation of the past—the good parts of Volvos past had been retained—and a harbinger of the future, establishing fundamental styling, or perhaps design is a better word, elements that have continued at least through 1993.

1967-1969

Although making its debut in 1966, production of the 144 did not get under way until early 1967, and American customers were able to buy the car as early as March. There was a choice of either a four-speed manual or three-speed automatic transmission, but for the United States the only engine was the 115bhp B18B. Domestic models came in either B18A (85bhp) or B18B versions, designated

1967 144S	
Dimensions	
Wheelbase	102.4in
Track	53.1/53.1in
Length	182.7in
Width	68.1in
Height	56.7in
Weight	2,545lb
Engine	
Type	Ohv I-4
Bore & stroke	3.31x3.15in (84.1x80.0mm)
Displacement	109ci (1778cc)
Compression	10.0:1
Fuel delivery	Two SU (1V)
Horsepower	115bhp @ 6000rpm
Torque	112lb-ft @ 4000rpm
Chassis and Drivetrain	
Layout, engine/drivetrain	F/R
Frame/body	Unit steel
Transmission	Four-speed manual
Rear axle ratio	4.10:1
Suspension, F/R	A-arm/live axle
Tires	165S-15
Brakes	Disc/disc
Performance	
0-60mph	12.3sec
1/4 mile	19.6sec @ 74mph
Fuel mileage	20–25mpg
Top speed	103mph

Production version of the 164E—photographed in its natural environment, a university faculty parking lot. The model differed little from the prototype except for vent grilles replacing the driving lights.

Volvo showed off the classically styled front end of the 164 in this 1969 ad that persuaded readers that they'd be thought to be rich if they drove a car like this.

144 and 144S respectively. All US models therefore carried the S designator.

A lighter and cheaper two-door variant, called 142 and 142S depending on engine, appeared in June, and the 145 station wagon somewhat later in the year. The new numbering system was simple: The first number indicated model, the second the number of cylinders, and the third the number of doors, plus a suffix for special equipment, if any.

Like *Star Trek*'s Mr. Spock, the Volvo 140 series was logical, if not exciting. The four-cylinder engine produced reasonable acceleration with reasonable fuel economy; the double A-arm front suspension and live rear axle on coil springs wasn't exotic but produced predictable handling and a comfortable ride.

The three-box profile contained a roomy passenger compartment with chair-like seats and a glassy, airy passenger compartment. The trunk was big, and both the rear and front box were designed to collapse in a controlled manner in a collision, a safety feature (the value of which was still debated at the time) that was available on Mercedes-Benz.

Volvo hoped most customers might avoid testing that controlled crush firsthand, however, by installing four-wheel disc brakes, unusual if not unique in the price class, and a split-triangle dual-circuit brake system that left 80 percent of braking force available if one circuit failed.

In the fall of 1967 (for the 1968 model year) changes were made to the exhaust system, wipers, and rearview mirror, and more padding was added to the seats. This was the P Series 140, the first 140s being the M Series. Cars sold in the United States saw their first exhaust emission controls, at this time simply preheating the air-fuel mixture in a complex intake manifold.

In the fall of 1968 (1969 models), the S Series got a needed power boost with the B20 series motor—critics had bashed the 140 for a perceived lack of pep. The B20A, with a single Zenith-Stromberg carburetor, was rated at 90bhp, while the B20B in the S-suffix cars (including all US-bound cars) made 118bhp. Though this was only three more horsepower, the wider, beefier torque curve made for a more pleasant car to drive.

An oil-type clutch kept the cooling fan speed below 3000rpm, reducing engine noise, and the cars were fitted with alternators. Cloth fabric for the seats was neither as slippery nor as hot to sit on in hot weather as the plastic surface had been. The only way to identify the new 2.0-liter Volvos was the B-20 badge on an otherwise plain grille.

The B20 engine wasn't the only news of autumn 1968. Volvo entered a new class of automobile with a larger, more luxurious model called the 164. As the numbers would suggest, this was basically a 140 series Volvo with a six-cylinder engine and four doors. The inline six was what today would be called modular, the B20 with two more cylinders added. Cylinder dimensions were the same, as were pistons, valves, connecting rods, and so forth. The block, as an extension of the five-main-bearing four, had seven main bearings.

The B30 engine, with two SU carburetors (Zenith-Strombergs in the United States), produced 145bhp at 5500rpm, making it quicker in 0–60mph, as *Car and Driver* pointed out, than the Mercedes 250 or the

1969 164	
Dimensions	
Wheelbase	106.3in
Track	53.1/53.1in
Length	185.6in
Width	68.3in
Height	56.7in
Weight	2,920lb
Engine	
Type	Ohv I-6
Bore & stroke	3.50x3.15in (89x80mm)
Displacement	182ci (2979cc)
Compression	9.2:1
Fuel delivery	Two Zenith-Stromberg CDSE (1V)
Horsepower	145bhp @ 5500rpm
Torque	163lb-ft @ 3300rpm
Chassis and Drivetrain	
Layout, engine/drivetrain	F/R
Frame/body	Unit steel
Transmission	Four-speed manual
Rear axle ratio	3.73:1
Suspension, F/R	A-arm/live axle
Tires	6.85x15in
Brakes	Disc/disc
Performance	
0-60mph	9.5sec
1/4 mile	17.6sec @ 83mph
Fuel mileage	17.5mpg
Top speed	110mph

Oldsmobile 98 even with the 455ci V-8. A ZF-made four-speed manual transmission was standard, with overdrive optional, and a three-speed automatic could also be had. Power steering from ZF was optional everywhere but the United States, where it was standard.

The longer engine of the 164 needed more room, and therefore the wheelbase was stretched 4in, the overall length growing by 3in, all of it ahead of the cowl. From there back, the body of the 164 was identical to the 144. Most striking, however, was the classic grille Volvo put on the 164, complete with the diagonal band and Volvo logo.

Inside, the fittings were more luxurious than the four-cylinder Volvo sedans, with carpeting, extra sound insulation, leather seat upholstery (originally cloth, but changed by the time cars were shipped to the United States), and fake wood glued to the dash which was otherwise like the 140 Series. A welcome switch was the location of a shorter shift lever back by the seats, rather than Volvo's truck-length lever still used in the 140s.

The 1970 model year was the last for the original grille design for the 142S. Driving lamps and overriders are nonstock accessories. Owner is Tom Jugus.

Dash of the 1970 142S has sixties-style speedometer, but with a Volvo safety gimmick—a driver-settable pointer to remind the driver not to drive too fast. Note the long shift lever—still.

1970-1971

The 1970 models, announced in the fall of 1969, saw safety detail improvements, including front-seat headrests and rear seat-belts, a day-night rearview mirror, and hazard warning flashers; an electrically heated rear window also was added, flow-through ventilation was moved to the C-pillar instead of the rear door seals (which hadn't worked well), and a rear window wiper became standard on the 145.

All 145 models originally had five side windows. The front door had both a vent window and normal wind-down glass. The back door had a single wind-down plane. The luggage compartment glass, however, had two panes of glass, the rearmost opening for ventilation. This continued through 1970,

Rear end of the 1972 142E typifies the simple styling of the 140 Series cars. The plastic trim around the taillights, originally "chrome," turned to tan so quickly many people think that's the way it was supposed to be.

changing in 1971 to a single fixed pane of glass at the rear, a passenger compartment exhaust vent having been added to the rear quarter panel.

For 1971, the wheelbase for all 140 Series cars was increased by 2cm to allow for fitting optional tires, the 15in wheels were made a half inch wider to 5.0in, and the front brake discs were bigger. The radiator was 25 percent larger as well, and openings were made in the panel below the front bumper. A new grille improved the front end's appearance over the original simple stamping.

Base model 140s got upholstery changes, but the excitement for 1971 was Volvo's new 142E sport sedan (called Grand Luxe—later GL—at home). The B20E engine, previously reserved for the 1800E, was installed in the two-door sedan and a 4.33:1 rear axle substituted for the 4.10:1 otherwise fitted. The M40 gearbox from the 164 was installed, complete with the Laycock de Normanville overdrive.

Second front-end design for 140 Series had the headlamps in separate pods and a black grille with diagonal slash. This 1970 142E is owned by Charles and Eileen Baldwin.

The 142E also had Pirelli 165 section radials instead of the standard bias-ply tires. To give an idea how far we've come, *Road & Track* called the 142E's 0.649g skidpad showing "a good account of itself."

The six-cylinder sedan joined the electronic revolution as well, the 164E becoming the most powerful Volvo automobile ever, rated at 175bhp on the home market but only 138bhp in the United States. A 164E badge on the tail differentiated the fuel-injected from the carbureted 164 (with 120 federalized horses) which was still sold in the States but not in California.

US federal requirements put a box beneath the dash that buzzed angrily until front seat occupants buckled up. Volvo put it on all models sold worldwide.

1972

Flush exterior door handles went on all 140 models and the 164, and the long gear

This mid-series 142 is in European trim. Note the lack of DOT side marker lights. *Volvo*

INTRODUCING THE VOLVO 142E. "WHAT'LL SHE DO?" "OH, ABOUT 11 YEARS."

Anybody can slap a big engine in a production sedan and call it a "GT."
Resulting in a car that disintegrates faster than anything on the street because it wasn't designed to handle all that power in the first place.

At Volvo, that isn't our idea of what a high performance car should be. So we're introducing the 142E. When you buy the 142E (Electronic fuel injection) you don't just get a hot engine in a standard production Volvo. You also get a bigger, stronger 4-speed transmission with overdrive. (Automatic is optional.) A tougher rear end. Larger 4-wheel power disc brakes. And wider wheels with radial tires.

And instead of being stripped down for racing, it's padded for comfort. The bucket seats for example, are covered in leather. And they're adjustable in a multitude of ways.

Above all, the 142E is a Volvo. And Volvos are built to last. Exactly how long we can't guarantee. But we do know Volvos last an average of eleven years in Sweden.

We know of no other high performance car that goes that slow.

Even for its factory hot rod, Volvo advertised longevity over speed—which even in 1971 wasn't fast compared to American muscle cars. Note lack of hubcaps.

The rear door on the 145 (and later station wagons) opened hatch-style. Note the ventilation exhaust vent on the quarter panel; it was placed below the rear window on sedans.

Nicely customized 1971 145S sports wheels from later-series Volvo, air dam, black-out trim, and Weber downdraft carburetor conversion on engine.

1971 142E	
Dimensions	
Wheelbase	103.1in
Track	53.1/53.1in
Length	182.7in
Width	68.3in
Height	57.7in
Weight	2,695lb
Engine	
Type	Ohv I-4
Bore & stroke	3.50x3.15in (89x80mm)
Displacement	121ci (1980cc)
Compression	10.5:1
Fuel delivery	Bosch K-Jetronic injection
Horsepower	130bhp @ 6000rpm
Torque	133lb-ft @ 3500rpm
Chassis and Drivetrain	
Layout, engine/drivetrain	F/R
Frame/body	Unit steel
Transmission	Four-speed manual plus overdrive
Rear axle ratio	4.33:1
Suspension, F/R	A-arm/live axle
Tires	165SR-15
Brakes	Disc/disc
Performance	
0-60mph	10.5sec
1/4 mile	17.5sec @ 76mph
Fuel mileage	23.7mpg
Top speed	106mph

Modified Swedish 164 proves "hot rod" translates to all languages!

lever in the 140 finally was replaced with a shorter, more modern lever. Other changes were minor details. That is, except for the bad news that the roll-back of compression ratios (to 8.7:1 for all engines) to meet federal emission rules knocked the wind out of

Lumbar adjuster on the front seat of a 1972 142E, an unusual luxury on an inexpensive model.

power output: The base 140s dropped to 97hp. The B20E engine in the 1800E and ES and the 142E lost 23hp, all the way down to 107hp, less than the base model of the year before. The Zenith-Stromberg carbureted 164 lost 25hp and was no longer available in

Finally, a shifter—on the 1972 142E—you don't have to be a truck driver to love.

A 1972 142E with the low-compression, fuel-injected B20F engine.

The 1971–1972 145 sported an optional luggage rack, as if the cavernous interior didn't provide enough carrying capacity. Note mileage badge on grille.

An optional gauge package for the 140 Series put a tachometer in the center of the dash.

California. The only good news was the addition of the 164E to the line.

The 140 Series cars sold west of the Mississippi River were equipped with fuel injection, riding on California's coattails. So in 1972 the 142E was accompanied by the 144E and 145E in western states, but all were low-performance low-compression engines.

For the rest of the world, the electronic fuel-injected six would be the most powerful Volvo automobile engine ever, producing 175bhp. But for the United States its output was limited to 138hp, less than the carbureted 1971 version. It was the first act of a struggle to maintain horsepower, fuel economy, and even legality that all manufacturers would endure in the face of ever-tightening emission rules during the dismal decade of the seventies.

1973

Bad news struck again in 1973 with the newly required safety bumpers—called

Racing 142s. Both are 1972 142Es for International Motor Sports Association (IMSA) small sedan series, the white car circa 1974; the black car competing from 1976 through 1983, after which it was made obsolete by a rule change specifying front-drive only. *iPd*

A pair of Volvos at Portland International Raceway in 1972, the 142 equipped with rare European accessory grille with integral driving lights. Both cars have iPd suspension kits and front spoilers.

Final 140 series grille was used in 1973 and 1974, although a new crash bumper was added in 1974.

"enormous (and ugly)" by *Road & Track*—that marred the appearance of all Volvos, while similar but invisible side guard beams went into the doors. Enthusiasts applauded a much improved dash, however, with circular, easy-to-read instruments and a higher-numerically first-gear ratio that allowed for quicker acceleration from rest.

Horsepower edged upward slightly for the fuel-injected 2.0 liter engines, and the carbureted engine disappeared from Volvo's US product line forever. The 164 was dropped, only the 164E being continued, and the 142E designation was eliminated as the

The big bumper on this 142 found in Granna, Sweden, identifies it as a 1974; federal "safety" bumpers were used on Volvos worldwide. Note headlamp wipers.

142, 144, and 145 became fuel injected nationwide. Visual changes included a new grille, front signal lights, and taillights. Volvo installed childproof locks on the rear doors.

The 1974 140 Series would be the last of the line, and the most apparent change was ventless front side windows, though the fuel tank was moved for safety and all automatic-transmission cars came equipped with power steering. For the United States, Volvo combined luxury appointments from the 164 with the four-cylinder chassis, dubbing the result the 142GL and 144GL (mechanically identical to the cheaper models). Bosch's mechanically timed K-Jetronic fuel injection was substituted for Bosch's electronic system, power falling to 109hp in the process.

The 164E was retained essentially unchanged for 1974, and along with the 140 Series, was replaced in Europe in 1975 with the 240/260 Series. Although the 240 crossed the Atlantic in 1975, the 164 was carried over for American consumption.

What to Look For

The 140 Series aren't old enough to be "old" yet, and many of them are still being used for day-to-day transportation. You can still pick up a 140 for used car prices and have a classic Volvo that's a lot of fun.

The 164s are similarly low priced, but were produced in lower numbers and are rarer and therefore it's more difficult to find a good one. With more luxury touches—the

Rear bumpers grew in 1974 as well, as shown on this 164E.

With power, even for Volvo, a memory by 1974, Volvo advertised its four-wheel disc brakes—which worked so that the big bumper didn't get any uglier than it already was.

140s are, with a few exceptions, rather Spartan—and more horsepower from its half again bigger engine, the 164 is a good bet for an enjoyable collectible.

One benefit of the 140/160 Series is interchangeability of major pieces such as glass and doors through the 240 Series all the way, at least, to 1992; doorhandles and latches may not be identical, however. Also, the rear doors of the station wagon are interchangeable with those of the four-door sedan.

Like the 1800s, the 140/160 Series comes in carbureted and fuel-injected versions. Of the carbureted cars, those with SU carbs are generally preferred. The Zenith-Strombergs are much more difficult to adjust and require special tools. The Bosch D-Jetronic fuel injection in the 140s is subject to the same problems as in the 1800, mainly deterioration of the wiring with age. It takes some troubleshooting to find which wire is defective.

The 164 uses the M400 (four-speed) or M410 (four-speed plus overdrive) manual transmission, different from the M40 and M41 (four-speed and four-speed plus overdrive respectively) transmission of the 140 Series. In spite of having more torque capacity than the transmission for the fours, the

Bumper laws in the United States required a massive front bumper and shortening of the grille on the 164 for 1974.

164 gearbox can be more of a problem when it comes to finding parts. Solenoids for the overdrive seem to last about 60,000 miles, although that's extremely variable. Second-gear synchros will suffer if the car has been driven hard, and repair runs about $300.

Some have reported the Borg-Warner BW35 three-speed automatic is not as durable as the later BW55, while others report no problems. The automatic, however, saps more horsepower than you probably want to give up, and a manual is preferable from this standpoint. The manual with overdrive is preferred as well, cutting noise and engine wear on the road and yielding improved gas mileage too.

The 142E of 1971 is the hot rod of the 140 series. This was the only year to combine fuel injection and a 10.5:1 compression ratio for the 142 (the same engine as the 1800E), the compression ratio falling to 8.7:1 in 1972 as emission requirements stiffened and under-hood horses died. The 142E of 1972 was a shadow of the previous year's.

Volvo changed the B20 engine in 1974. One of the changes was to stouter-looking connecting rods that in practice were not as strong. Some Volvo enthusiasts won't touch these engines at all, while others consider them sturdy for everything short of competition use. Used in 1974 and 1975, these final (for the United States) B20 engines can be identified by the auxiliary air valve on the intake manifold instead of on the head, or eight bolts on the rear end of the crankshaft (this cannot be seen unless the engine is out of the car, of course).

Overall, the 140 Series and 164 cars have a lot to recommend them. They are light and nimble, have four-wheel disc brakes, and have reasonable power. The 1971 142E is considered a good pick for the Sports Car Club of America's (SCCA) Improved Touring-B class (for any track without a "freeway"). As Volvos, they are extremely durable and easily go 200,000 miles without serious attention, as long as they've received regular maintenance and exposure to salt has been limited. And the price is still low. They may never be megabuck values, but they'll never be this cheap again.

Photo of a prototype 164 shows the classic grille and longer front end appended to what is otherwise a 144. *Volvo*

$^1/_2$	**242, 244, 245 (1975 only)**
★	**242, 244, 245 DL GL, GLT**
	(non Turbo)
$^1/_2$	**264, 265, GLE**
$^1/_2$	**Diesel**
★★★	**242GT**
★★	**GLT Turbo, Turbo**

240 and 260 Series 1974-Current

A Car, A Tradition

That the Volvo 240, making its debut in the 1975 model year, was new is undeniable, but to say that it was "All New" is not true at all. In fact, from the cowl back it was virtually identical to the 140. Only from the firewall forward were changes made. Those were, however, substantial enough to warrant the new name.

Most obvious was the new grille. For the 240, this was a backward slanting affair reminiscent of the Volvo ESV "safety car." *Car and Driver* reported that even Volvo insiders considered it ugly. Across the grille was the traditional Volvo slash with the Volvo badge centered on it.

Important but less visible changes included MacPherson struts (for more under-hood room for an anticipated proliferation of emission controls) and rack and pinion steering. Wheel diameter dropped to 14in, though wider-section-width 185 tires were also fitted; steel-belted radials were standard on all models.

For one last year in the United States, power would be the pushrod B20E (a new 2.1 liter engine was available in 1975 only in Europe where, it was noted, it would be easier to fix any problems). Tightening emission regulations sapped horsepower, Californians losing the most. Volvo put in a lower first gear (higher ratio numerically) for snappier acceleration, though as *Road & Track* noted, it helped only until second gear. Overdrive, engaged by a button on the shift lever, helped fuel economy and made for

The 240 Series came with Volvo ESV-inspired grille from 1975 through 1977. Both US and European 240 series had round headlamps and shared grille design for this period. Owner is James Brown.

quieter cruising. Breakerless ignition, hardened valve seats, a stronger starter motor, and larger radiator were new features for 1975, and California cars got catalytic converters. Two-door, four-door, and five-door wagons were, respectively, the 242, 244, and 245, with standard DL and upgrade GL versions. Note that "California cars" meant all cars distributed west of the Mississippi River at this time; these cars got lower power ratings than cars distributed from the East Coast—at least from 1976.

Note how the rear side door interchangeability with the sedan was maintained on the 245 wagon. *Volvo*

1976

The 240 Series was back for 1976 basically unchanged but for the new B21F engine. And what a change! Much more than a mere displacement increase, the new 2127cc engine had a belt-driven overhead cam, the cylinder head itself now aluminum with a cross-flow design. Both horsepower and torque were improved, with peak torque at a lower rpm for better drivability. The catalytic converter was combined with Volvo's new Lambda Sond control system for California cars. With the new engine, said *Road & Track*, "The car has flair and is not just getting by anymore."

The 260 Series made its US debut in 1976, having been sold in Europe the previous year. The front end of the series stayed with the classic theme of the 164, with a bright vertical-bar grille adapted to the 5mph bumper below it. US buyers, however, got quad sealed-beam headlamps instead of the large rectangular lamps with washer-wiper of the Euro-spec model. A less obvious change was the reduction of the 260 Series wheelbase to that of the 240, both now with wheels 104in apart.

The shorter front end of the 264 was made possible by the replacement of the trusty Volvo inline six with a V-6 made in

But for the new front end, the 244 would resemble its predecessors.

1975 242GL	
Dimensions	
Wheelbase	104in
Track	55.9/53.1in
Length	192.6in
Width	67.1in
Height	56.5in
Weight	3,090lb
Engine	
Type	Ohv I-4
Bore & stroke	3.50x3.15in (88.9x80.0mm)
Displacement	121ci (1990cc)
Compression	8.7:1
Fuel delivery	Bosch K-Jetronic injection
Horsepower	94bhp @ 6000rpm
Torque	105lb-ft @ 3500rpm
Chassis and Drivetrain	
Layout, engine/drivetrain	F/R
Frame/body	Unit steel
Transmission	Four-speed manual plus overdrive
Rear axle ratio	4.30:1
Suspension, F/R	Strut/live axle
Tires	185-14
Brakes	Disc/disc
Performance	
0-60mph	14.2sec
1/4 mile	20.1sec @ 70mph
Fuel mileage	18.5mpg
Top speed	95mph

France as a Peugeot-Renault-Volvo joint venture. The all-aluminum ninety-degree six had a chain-driven overhead cam for each bank, each operating valves via rocker arms on a shaft above the camshaft, allowing the valves to be splayed in the semi-hemispherical combustion chambers. Continuous-flow Bosch injection and pointless electronic ignition were used on the new engine, again only California-bound models getting catalytic converters.

1977–1978

The following year saw only minor mechanical and trim changes, and for 1978 the exclusive 262 Coupe was available in the United States.

Something else to cheer about in 1978, especially for enthusiasts, was the 242GT. Stating that Volvos since the introduction of the 144 in 1966 were "for people who didn't like cars very much," David E. Davis, Jr., found the 242GT "a Volvo even a car lover could love . . . one that fairly shouts for attention and has no qualms about getting flogged around your favorite back roads."

The 240 Series received new grilles in 1978, American market cars getting essentially the same grille as the 260 Series. The Euro market 240 Series had the chrome strip moved from around the parking lights to inside. Rectangular lamps came to the 1979 Euro GL and GLE, while the less-expensive DL got square lamps.

1976 264GL	
Dimensions	
Wheelbase	103.9in
Track	55.9/53.2in
Length	192.9in
Width	67.2in
Height	56.5in
Weight	3,248lb
Engine	
Type	Sohc V-6
Bore & stroke	3.46x2.87in (88x73mm)
Displacement	162ci (2664cc)
Compression	8.2:1
Fuel delivery	Bosch K-Jetronic injection
Horsepower	125bhp @ 5500rpm
Torque	150lb-ft @ 2750rpm
Chassis and Drivetrain	
Layout, engine/drivetrain	F/R
Frame/body	Unit steel
Transmission	Four-speed manual plus overdrive
Rear axle ratio	3.73:1
Suspension, F/R	Strut/live axle
Tires	185R-14
Brakes	Disc/disc
Performance	
0-60mph	10.2sec
¼ mile	17.9sec @ 75.3mph
Fuel mileage	17–22mpg
Top speed	103mph

Bureaucratic entanglements kept the iPd turbo kit off the market until the factory turbo came out, eliminating demand for the iPd kit. This iPd-modified 1977 240 turbo was featured in *Road & Track*.

65

The 242GT was as exciting as it got in 1979 and 1980. Special wheels, side stripes, and an air dam were matched by a grille from the original 1975 242 modified for driving lights. Horsepower? Only 107. *Volvo*

Available in any color as long as it was silver with black and orange stripes, the 242GT came with stiffer front and rear springs and shocks and a larger front antiroll bar.

1978 242GT	
Dimensions	
Wheelbase	104in
Track	56.7/53.0in
Length	192.6in
Width	67.2in
Height	56.2in
Weight	2,930lb
Engine	
Type	Sohc I-4
Bore & stroke	3.62x3.15in (92x80mm)
Displacement	130ci (2127cc)
Compression	8.5:1
Fuel delivery	Bosch K-Jetronic injection
Horsepower	101bhp @ 5200rpm
Torque	111lb-ft @ 2500rpm
Chassis and Drivetrain	
Layout, engine/drivetrain	F/R
Frame/body	Unit steel
Transmission	Four-speed manual plus overdrive
Rear axle ratio	3.91:1
Suspension, F/R	Strut/live axle
Tires	185/70HR-14
Brakes	Disc/disc
Performance	
0-60mph	11.3sec
1/4 mile	18.5sec @ 75mph
Fuel mileage	20mpg
Top speed	109mph

All United States 242GTs came equipped with the California-specification engine. This meant that east of the Mississippi River, standard 242s were actually faster than their more sporting siblings. In other markets, a high-compression 140hp B23E engine was used in the 242GT but sadly never brought to the United States.

A special grille, complete with foglights and trendy black trim and a pinstriped chin spoiler were distinctive, and Pirelli CN36 185/70HR-14 radials mounted on 14x5in 1/2J cast-alloy wheels completed the look. The GT was one of the fastest cars around *Road & Track*'s skidpad at 0.754g and through the slalom as well. Ride was firm, but not objectionable. The engine, however, was called underwhelming for a car labeled GT, and in fact it was only the standard 240 Series four-banger, smog-choked to 101bhp (California rating) and 11.3 seconds in the 0–60mph dash.

New faces for the 240 and 260 Series also marked the 1978 model year. For the 240s, the two-door cars would get horizontal black-bar grilles, while the four-doors and wagons got quad round headlamps with raised vertical-bar grille similar to the 260 Series. The 260s, meanwhile, had front ends freshened with quad rectangular lamps.

Striped black corduroy seats, tachometer, small-diameter steering wheel, and a short-throw shifter made the 242GT interior special. Three-point belts in the back seat were already standard equipment. *Volvo*

1979

Changes for 1979 were limited. In addition to minor trim changes, the trunk opening was changed for easier loading and there was a new one-piece (but multi-colored) taillight assembly. Wagons got easier-closing gas-strut supports for the tailgate.

All sedans but the GT acquired heavier antiroll bars front and rear (front from 18.0 to 19.5mm, and rear 16.0 to 19.0mm). The wagon's front bar received a similar increase, while at the rear a bar (16.0mm) was installed for the first time. The GT changed from 21/18 to 21/23. Stiffer shocks were fitted as well, and fully automatic self-leveling shocks went on the rear of the 265 station wagon. Caster was increased, and improvements were made to ventilation and air conditioning, the 260 models getting thermostatic control.

1980

For the United States, 1980 saw some interesting, if not thrilling, changes. To begin with, the model lines were simplified. First was the DL, previously known as the 242. The new GL combined the front end and higher trim level of the 264GL with the four-cylinder engine. The 264GL became the GLE, while the 262C became simply the Coupe.

The 242GT became simply the GT, although antiroll bars were changed yet again,

1980 Diesel	
Dimensions	
Wheelbase	104in
Track	55.9/53.1in
Length	192.5in
Width	67.3in
Height	56.5in
Weight	3,300lb
Engine	
Type	Sohc I-6
Bore & stroke	3.0x3.4in (76.5x86.4mm)
Displacement	145.4ci (2383cc)
Compression	23.5:1
Fuel delivery	Bosch mechanical
Horsepower	78bhp @ 4800rpm
Torque	102lb-ft @ 3000rpm
Chassis and Drivetrain	
Layout, engine/drivetrain	F/R
Frame/body	Unit steel
Transmission	Four-speed manual plus overdrive
Rear axle ratio	3.54:1
Suspension, F/R	Strut/live axle
Tires	185/70SR-14
Brakes	Disc/disc
Performance	
0-60mph	18.5sec
1/4 mile	21.2sec @ 64.5mph
Fuel mileage	28mpg (EPA)
Top speed	N/A

The Garret TB03 turbocharger boosted (pun intended) Volvo's 2.1 liter four to 127hp. The new B21FT engine was modified inside, but the turbo application had the appearance of a kit, unlike today's integrated systems. *Volvo*

this time to 23/21 front and rear, and gas-filled shocks were used. Visible changes on the GT included Pirelli P-6 tires on new five-spoke 6x15in alloy wheels, a new front spoiler and GT instead of 242GT on the trunklid.

The V-6 in the 260 Series got a boost in displacement from 2664 to 2849cc, with a concurrent designation change to B28F. Horsepower increased marginally from 127 to 130bhp at 5500rpm, torque also rising from 146 to 153lb-ft at 2750rpm.

Lastly (in more ways than one), a diesel-engined Volvo became available in the United States, basically the 240 Series with a Volkswagen-built inline six-cylinder oilburner. With only 76hp, acceleration was, not surprisingly, glacier-like. A wagon tested by *Car and Driver* took 18.2 seconds to go from 0–60mph.

1981

Volvo became the largest European car exporter to the United States in 1981, and better yet, the turbocharged engine introduced in Europe the year before crossed the Atlantic for American consumption. This Garret TB03-equipped B21FT made 127

The new GLT of 1981 came in Turbo form for the two-door sedan or nonturbo for the station wagon. *Volvo*

The 1981 264 was distinguished by silver vertical bars in the grille and quad rectangular headlamps (one large rectangular lamp per side in Europe); the 240 Series had black vertical bars and round lamps. *Volvo*

Seats in the 1981 264GL could pass for living room furniture and were arguably more comfortable, with adjustable height and lumbar support. Driver's seat was heated. *Volvo*

The GLT line was extended to include station wagons in 1981, but not with the turbocharged engine. *Volvo*

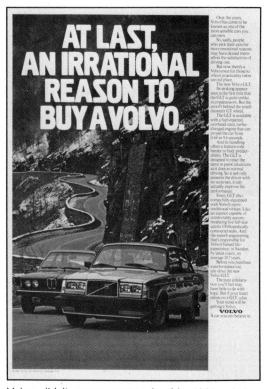

Volvo didn't name names in this 1981 ad, but everyone knows that's a BMW 528 being passed by a Volvo GLT.

All 1981 Volvos received an updated dash with large gauges and cubby, which Volvo said could be used for storage or fitted with an accessory gauge cluster. *Volvo*

"stout Swedish horses"—per factory literature—at 5400rpm and 150lb-ft of torque at 3750rpm in the GLT Turbo, the runner of the new GLT line that replaced the GT.

Not merely a hang-on turbo kit, changes to the engine included compression dropped from 9.3:1 to 7.5:1, sodium-cooled valves with Stellite seats and faces, and a one-quart thermostatically controlled oil cooler. The turbo cars also got the ventilated disc brakes from the six-cylinder cars, a lower first gear, and taller final drive.

Stylewise, the GLT Turbo got the grille and hood similar to the GL but with the center blacked out. Color choices were silver, metallic red, or black. For 1981, the GLT Turbo was available only in two-door sedan form.

The GLT was also available without turbocharger, featuring the same styling, wheels, tires, and suspension as the GLT Turbo, which carried these items over from the 1980 GT. Nonturbo GLTs—two-door sedan or five-door wagon(!)—came with the 107hp B21F four. Color choices for the GLT two door were metallic red or silver. The GLT wagon was available in four metallic colors; a limited-edition anniversary model came in silver with blue velour interior.

All Volvos got a new panoramic dash with storage cubbies, the GLT Turbo getting an extra gauge package including turbocharger boost, oil pressure, and volt gauges. The new two-door version of the GL became available, but changes to both DL and GLE were limited to halogen high beams, new window trim, and such. The four-speed plus overdrive manual transmission no longer

Boost gauge was part of the full instrumentation on the GLT Turbo. *Volvo*

New taillights went on wagons in 1981, which were available with either gas or diesel power. *Volvo*

came on the GLE, however; only a three-speed automatic was available.

1982

Volvo answered the obvious question in 1982, offering the turbocharged B21FT engine in the station wagon, creating in the GLT Turbo five-door "a wagon that really hauls," per the company's public relations department. A four-door GLT turbo was also added, rounding out the line.

The nonturbo GLTs (and some California DL four-doors) came equipped with Volvo's new-for-1982 B21FLH engine, basically the 2.1 liter four with Bosch microprocessor-controlled L-Jetronic fuel injection. The new engine was rated at 105bhp, compared to

This 1981 GLT Turbo was modified with an iPd styling kit, wheels, and European headlamps. It also had a pre-factory intercooler created by iPd. *iPd*

Another variation on the Volvo theme is this 245 (or 265?) commercial high-roof wagon seen in Stockholm, Sweden.

The DL was the mainstream model for Volvo in 1982. *Volvo*

98bhp for the B21F. Nonturbo GLT availability, however, was reduced to the two-door model only.

Diesels were more available, with full fifty-state availability and in DL, GL, and wagon configuration.

A new four-speed automatic replaced the three-speed self-shifter for all but the diesel engine. Fourth gear was actually a 31 percent overdrive and could be locked out, for reduced shifting in traffic, by a button on top of the floor-mounted gearshift. Electronic ignition was added for the B21F engine, and all but the diesels got a new seventy-amp alternator.

1983

Volvo's big news for 1983 was the introduction of the 760 GLE as its flagship model. The immediate effect was the elimination of the 240/260 Series-based GLE, the DL, GL, and GLT models continuing. However, the B21F engine was replaced by the B23F, basically a bored-out version of the original,

Volvo put available parts together and made the GLT Turbo "five-door" and called it "a wagon that really hauls." Nobody else had anything like it in 1982. *Volvo*

The GLE continued in 1982 with a bright grille, V-6 engine, and four-door model only. *Volvo*

Volvos have served as police cars and taxi cabs in upscale neighborhoods like Falls Church, Virginia. *Volvo*

though now with Bosch LH electronic injection instead of Bosch continuous fuel injection.

Compression was also raised, although

two versions of the engine, for manual and automatic transmissions, had different specifications. The manual transmission engine had a 9.5:1 compression ratio and made

1982 GLT Turbo

Dimensions
Wheelbase	104.3in
Track	56.3/53.5in
Length	192.5in
Width	67.3in
Height	56.2in
Weight	3,070lb

Engine
Type	Sohc I-4
Bore & stroke	3.62x3.15in (92x80mm)
Displacement	130ci (2131cc)
Compression	7.5:1
Fuel delivery	Bosch K-Jetronic injection
Horsepower	127bhp @ 5400rpm
Torque	150lb-ft @ 3750rpm

Chassis and Drivetrain
Layout, engine/drivetrain	F/R
Frame/body	Unit steel
Transmission	Four-speed manual plus overdrive
Rear axle ratio	3.73:1
Suspension, F/R	Strut/live axle
Tires	195/60HR-15
Brakes	Disc/disc

Performance
0-60mph	10.2sec
1/4 mile	17.4sec @ 78.5mph
Fuel mileage	20.5mpg
Top speed	114mph

An intercooler was standard equipment on Volvo Turbos built after December 1983, but the extra 30hp was available in a Volvo kit for earlier turbocharged models. Volvo promised 0-60mph in under eight seconds with the intercooler. *Volvo*

73

1983 Limited Edition 240 Turbo

If politics makes strange bedfellows—keep your prurient thoughts to yourself—then racing makes unusual variants available to car buyers. In particular this refers to what has become known as the 1983 Volvo Limited Edition 240 Turbo.

It is not described in any factory literature, and the name is merely customary. Special Edition is also used to describe the car. Volvo gave it no name and probably was reluctant to put anything into print lest it run afoul of the public, the government, or FISA, the international race sanctioning body.

The car in question was a special model for the European Touring Car Championship, which has a 5,000 car homologation mini-mum, though "evolution" models need a run of 500 cars only. Because fuel economy as well as power was important in this series, and because the Lambda Sond-equipped cars were the most fuel efficient, and because Lambda Sond cars were sold only in the North American market at the time, Volvo decided to homologate the cars in the United States.

And since the "flat hood" of the first-series 240 was more aerodynamic than the later "formal" grille, the car was homologized with that hood and the flat grille from the 1978–1980 European model, sprayed silver over its original black.

As prepped for the FISA inspection, the cars were equipped with a larger-than-standard turbocharger, the factory intercooler

Called flat hood or Special Edition, 500 late 1983 Turbos received an intercooler and special grilles and hoods as part of a race-car homologation scheme. *Michael Leslie/Northstar Photoworks*

that would not be available until midyear 1984, and a combination of cylinder head and intake manifold both rigged with fuel-injection jets in each; the manifold jets supplied a water-alcohol mix at boost pressures over 7psi. The modifications resulted in anything but a showroom stock racer: Volvo published specifications listing maximum power of 340hp at 6600rpm and maximum torque at 400lb-ft at 4000-6000rpm. Trunk-lid spoilers were also placed in the trunk of every car.

The cars were not sold this way, however. All the special equipment (exclusive of the body parts and intercooler) was removed—if in truth it had been installed—and the spoilers shipped back to Sweden. Volvo's logic, when FISA learned of the ruse, was that the cars needed only to be sold with the equipment (and they were, to the distributor), not delivered that way to the public.

Though it is unlikely that anyone would bogus a Limited Edition, Volvo outwardly identified the car as a 1983 GLT two-door; its window sticker had an extra line: "Intercooler and Trim Package, $995.00." You can, however, check the designation plate for an "SXXXXX" identifier.

Serial numbers are not consecutive, as the intercooler kits were installed after the cars were shipped to the United States and mixed in the port parking lot. Manual and automatic transmission versions were produced, and approximately half were distributed from each coast, which should not be taken to mean that none were sold by dealers in the Midwest.

What the Limited Edition cars are, then, are "early" intercooler cars, though with less flashy grilles. However, they do not have the larger clutch plate of the factory intercooler-equipped cars of 1984–1985, nor the thermostatically controlled electric fan for the radiator. Although the later cars are mechanically superior, the racing connection imbues them with extra panache and superior collectibility—but probably not as much as current owners would like. Be price wary on these cars.

Actual racers were significantly different from the 500 production Special Edition Turbos, however, as Volvo promotional photo shows. Note the spoiler on the trunk lid. *Volvo*

For 1984, turbocharger-equipped 240s could be had with two doors, called the Volvo Turbo . . . *Volvo*

. . . or with four doors, called the Volvo Turbo Four-Door . . . *Volvo*

. . . or with five doors, called the Volvo Turbo Wagon. All had a small Turbo badge on the grille and a larger one on the trunk. *Volvo*

111bhp, while the automatic transmission engine got a 10.3:1 compression ratio and 114bhp. This engine was available in the DL and GL 2.3 liter.

The diesel was still available in the GL 2.4 liter diesel and the 2.1 liter turbo B21FT in the GLT Turbo.

1984

The 760 Series had the effect of pushing the 240 Series out of the limelight, even though improvements continued to be offered. The turbo engine still displaced 2127cc, but an intercooler introduced midyear bumped power to 162bhp. The engine was now known as the B21FT/IBS, the suffix standing for Intercooler Boost System. At the same time, Volvo made a kit available to raise any earlier B21FT to IBS status.

Two-, four- and five-door models were available in DL, GL, and Turbo trim, with either manual or automatic transmission, as was the Diesel, except no two-door diesels could be had. For 1984, the DL got fancier trim previously reserved for the GL and a richer upholstery. Metallic paint was available as an option on the DL for the first time. The GLT designation was dropped for 1984, making 1983 the last year it was used.

And Volvo was perfectly willing to mention BMW in this 1984 advertisement.

1985

Two-door versions of the DL, GL, and Turbo were dropped for 1985 and the diesel was gone altogether. A new engine, the

240 Turbo Comparison

Year	Model	Horsepower	Torque	Weight	Acceleration	Quarter-Mile Time
1981	2dr	127 @ 5400rpm	150 @ 3750rpm	3,020lb	9.6sec	17.2sec @ 80mph*
1982	2dr	127 @ 5400rpm	150 @ 3750rpm	3,070lb	10.2sec	17.4sec @ 78.5mph**
	5dr	127 @ 5400rpm	150 @ 3750rpm	3,200lb	8.9sec	16.7sec @ 82mph*
1983	2dr	127 @ 5400rpm	150 @ 3750rpm	na	9.0sec	16.8sec @ 81mph*
	2dr w/IBS kit	157 @ 5100rpm	175 @ 3900rpm	na	7.9sec	15.8sec @ 87mph*
	2dr SE w/IBS	157 @ 5100rpm	175 @ 3900rpm	na	8.0sec	16.10sec @ 85.6mph
	5dr	127 @ 5400rpm	150 @ 3750rpm	na	na	na
1984	2dr IBS	162 @ 5100rpm	181 @ 2900rpm	2,990lb	8.85sec	16.70sec @ 84.2mph***
	4dr IBS	162 @ 5100rpm	181 @ 2900rpm	na	na	na
	5dr IBS	162 @ 5100rpm	181 @ 2900rpm	3,215lb	10.1sec	17.5sec @ 77mph**
1985	4dr IBS	162 @ 5100rpm	181 @ 2900rpm	3,045lb	na	na
	5dr IBS	162 @ 5100rpm	181 @ 2900rpm	3,157lb	na	na

*Car and Driver test
**Road & Track test
***Motor Trend test

The advent of the 700 Series relegated the 240 Series to a supporting role, but the 240GL of 1986 proved basic need not be Spartan: twenty-five-spoke alloy wheels, air conditioning, power windows and locks, and sunroof were all standard equipment. *Volvo*

B230F, replaced the B23F on DLs and GLs. The new engine produced 114bhp at 5400rpm and 136lb-ft of torque at 2750rpm, the low-torque peak yielding improved drivability. Volvo boasted the combined effect of new pistons, connecting rods, and crankshaft made less drag for better fuel economy and improved durability.

Rear foglights were added in 1985 and this was the year that the dreaded "upshift"

Evergreen 1989 240GL updated with aero headlamps—but the wagon still had doors interchangeable with a 1968 144! *Volvo*

light was added for manual transmission cars.

The Turbo continued as a four-door or five-door and with the older B21FT engine (which still had marginally more peak horsepower than the new B23FT turbo engine offered in the 700 Series, though less torque). It was the last year for a turbocharged 240, as the company concentrated more on the 700 Series.

1986

The attention to the 700 Series made it look like the 200 Series cars were on the way out, but continuing demand—plus well-amortized costs—made Volvo take another look at the junior model of its product line. For the 1986 model year, the line was freshened ("refined" is what Volvo called it).

The 240 designation was revived and applied to four-door and five-door versions, in both base DL and upscale GL trim.

The sheet metal was new from the firewall forward, with a longer hood and a lower, wider grille. Fenders were new as well, and large rectangular European-style headlamps were fitted. The trunk lid was revised, with a raised center section for reduced drag. A host of minor refinements inside and out completed the models' updating.

The engine and drivetrain, however, remained unchanged (though the turbo was dropped) with the B230F four-cylinder and choice of four-speed-plus-overdrive manual or four-speed automatic transmissions.

1987–1991

Changes to the 240 line were minimal through 1989, perhaps the most significant being the rear headrests installed that year. For 1990, the 240GL was dropped and the 240DL became the king of the less-expensive Volvos, a simple 240 becoming the entry-level Volvo on which air conditioning, radio, and power windows were options rather than standard equipment. Air bags, however, were on every 240 brought into the country. The only visible change was a new tailgate on the wagons with a larger flush-mounted window.

For 1991 even the DL was dropped, the line being unified under a simple 240 badge.

Air conditioning was standard, antilock brakes (ABS) optional. The B230F continued as the only engine available in all 240 models.

1992

Like a yo-yo the 240GL keeps going away and coming back, and for 1992 it returned to provide a list of luxury items as standard equipment, including a sunroof, power/ heated outside mirrors, rear shelf speakers, power antenna, and heated front seats. The GL, available as a sedan only, can be distinguished by a chrome grille and trim package from lesser 240s, which have a matte-black grille and trim.

All 240s for 1992 got ABS as standard equipment, all Volvos now so equipped. Other across-the-board improvements were an improved heat control valve, a larger-diameter front antisway bar, and revalved shock absorbers.

1993

Another year of evolutionary changes greeted the 240 Series in 1993. The 240 was available in four-door and five-door versions, and the upgrade model including in its extra price a sunroof, heated front seats, and power antenna. All 1993 models got CFC-free air conditioning, bigger fuel tanks, and upgraded audio. All 240s, instead of just the GL, got power mirrors. An automatic locking differential replaced a limited-slip differential as the extra-grip option.

What to Look For

The 240 Series is a living legend. Not many models introduced in 1975 are still in production, with no end seemingly in sight. Which is not to say the current 240 is the same as that of 1975. If it were, it wouldn't be here.

The 1975 240 is universally noted as a car to avoid by Volvo enthusiasts. A new, heavier

Joseph Nicolato, Volvo Cars of North America, says the market will determine how long the 240 stays on the market. A facelift freshened the 240 for yet another year in 1992. *Volvo*

(though stronger and safer) bodystyle was combined with the old B20 engine, burdened with emission controls and at a low point in power output since the introduction of fuel injection. Add to that the redesigned (and inferior) connecting rods introduced in 1974, and the 1975 240 is a car to avoid. Better to go with a 1976 and get the new and improved B21 engine.

An important note about the B21 and subsequent overhead-cam engines: These engines use a toothed belt for cam drive, which is completely reliable if it is cared for properly. Because it's a rubber belt, avoid contact with petroleum products which will cause deterioration. That includes your greasy, oily hands. It's also advisable to replace the belt if it has been removed for some reason, since it is not as strong as it was originally.

Also follow the replacement schedule. For pre-1986 gasoline engines, Volvo says replace the belt at 40,000 miles; for 1986 and later engines, change the belt at 50,000 miles. Diesels should have the belt replaced at 75,000. This is important because Volvo engines are not "freewheeling," that is, if the belt breaks, pistons will strike open valves and dollars will fly out of your wallet. If the belt looks bad before its due date, change it, and if it looks good despite the mileage, replace it anyway. Experts claim that external appearance can be deceiving.

The B27 V-6, which debuted in the North American market in the 1976 260 Series, is much maligned among Volvo enthusiasts, first because "it's not a Volvo engine" and second, because it has a history of poor valvetrain oiling and resultant wear. Volvo admits as much, with a kit to replace the camshafts by drilling holes in the firewall and drawing them out through the passenger compartment. The kit comes complete with hole saw and rubber plugs for the firewall, but it's a sad commentary on the engine itself. The B27 (and after the displacement increase, B28) was used in the 240 Series

through 1982 in the GLE, then dropped when the 700 Series took over luxury duty.

The turbocharged fours are a better bet, although the turbochargers have an average life of about 80,000 miles according to some sources. Of course, abused they can expire at 20,000 miles; they've also been known to last 150,000–160,000 miles. Water cooling the turbo bearings starting in 1987 increased turbo life to that of "engine lifetime," though that's academic to the 240 Series which lost the turbo version after 1985!

The Turbo of 1984 and 1985 were high-water marks of 240 Series performance: the GLT Turbo station wagon of 1982 only wins a special place in Volvo legend, having been successfully raced in SCCA competition. With 162hp in the relatively light 240 chassis, the GLT Turbo is capable of respectable performance even by current standards, especially for a five-passenger sedan.

The predecessor of the GLT was the GT, and although not the stormer the Turbo models were, these striped and spoilered sedans were an indication that the mundane seventies hadn't taken all the joy from Götenborg. The GT and GLT will carry a premium in price over other 240 Series cars, but are still affordable and a lot of fun for the dollar. These are keepers to find and save while they're still available and in good shape.

Alternatively, the V-6 in the 260 Series cars can be replaced by a Chevrolet or Ford V-8; several shops have specialized in this procedure that has no real negative effect on handling or fuel economy but dramatically improves acceleration, depending on the specific V-6. The Camaro driver in the next lane will never know what hit him. Of course, don't expect Volvo to honor your warranty!

Then again, there's the diesels. Unless you really need an excuse to visit truck stops, forget them. The turbodiesels have acceptable acceleration, but the naturally aspirated models are *slow, slow, slow,* and often smokey to boot.

262C 1977-1981

An Italian Suit For A Sturdy Swede

While the 260 Series had all the luxury any right-thinking person could want, it lacked that certain impracticality that marks a truly exclusive luxury automobile. Impracticality being in short supply at the Volvo factory, Volvo went to Italy and specifically the styling studio of Bertone for the new model that was to become its flagship in grandeur and elegance.

Priced in the same neighborhood as the Cadillac Eldorado and 5 Series BMW, the 1978 Volvo 262C debuted to a world that marveled at what apparently was a two-door 260 with what *Car and Driver* called "a top chop that would warm George Barris' heart."

Indeed, headroom—or the lack thereof —was the critics' biggest complaint. The roof was lowered 3.5in, and even dropping the

The 262C was either handsome or impractical, depending on your point of view. All 1978 cars came with the black vinyl top. *Volvo*

In 1980, the 262C became simply the Coupe and was available without the vinyl top. *Volvo*

The interior was still sumptuous—or gaudy, depending on your taste. Doors had pleated leather with elm inserts. *Volvo*

seats by 1.2in couldn't make up the difference. Volvo confessed to the low overhead but rationalized that "the Coupe was not designed to suit everyone." In addition to lowering the top, the C-pillar was widened, the windows reshaped, and the windshield reclined to a greater angle.

The $15,000-plus price tag was necessary if one was to finish the interior in soft, pleated "furniture-grade" leather and real elm veneer panels on the doors. Oddly, armrests and steering wheel were covered in plastic, and the dash, except for full instrumentation, was the same as even the humblest Volvo.

The powertrain, suspension, and even most of the body panels are right off the ordinary 260 Series cars. Such are the limitations of low volume. Of course, full equipment was standard, including power assists, air conditioning, and cruise control. Manual or automatic transmissions were available, though most came with the automatic.

For its first year the only color scheme available was silver with a black vinyl top, to be joined by gold over gold (no vinyl top) in 1979. By the final year, colors were gold or a pastel blue, neither with vinyl tops.

For 1980 there was a name change, the model simply being known as the Volvo Coupe and, like the rest of the 260 Series (which became the GLE in 1980), the V-6 engine was increased in displacement and redesignated as the B28F. Horsepower edged up to an even 130bhp. Changes for 1981 were limited to the new dash that the rest of the Volvo line received and heating elements in the right front seat (as on the GLE) so you can warm your passenger's buns as well as your own.

Volvo imported 750 262Cs in 1978, 1,500 coupes each in 1979 and 1980, and 750 in 1981. The Volvo Coupe was absent, however, from the 1982 line-up. Volvo would be moving upmarket with the 760 Series, and the Coupe, having served its purpose, was allowed to retire.

1978 262C	
Dimensions	
Wheelbase	104in
Track	56.3/53.5in
Length	192.5in
Width	67.3in
Height	53.9in
Weight	3,120lb
Engine	
Type	Sohc V-6
Bore & stroke	3.46x2.87in (88x73mm)
Displacement	162ci (2664cc)
Compression	8.2:1
Fuel delivery	Bosch K-Jetronic injection
Horsepower	125bhp @ 5750rpm
Torque	150lb-ft @ 2750rpm
Chassis and Drivetrain	
Layout, engine/drivetrain	F/R
Frame/body	Unit steel
Transmission	Four-speed manual plus overdrive
Rear axle ratio	3.73:1
Suspension, F/R	Strut/live axle
Tires	185/70SR-14
Brakes	Disc/disc
Performance	
0-60mph	11.1sec
1/4 mile	18.3sec @ 76.5mph
Fuel mileage	16.5mpg
Top speed	109mph

Brilliant white paint, full styling kit, custom wheels, and iPd suspension make this 1981 Coupe a standout—though it won't be loved by everyone. Killer stereo system and modified 1987 turbo four from 740 are hidden assets. Builder is Scott Hart. *iPd*

What to Look For

With only about 1,000 cars imported every year for its brief (especially for a Volvo) model run, there are relatively few 262C/Coupes out there, even allowing for a high Volvo survival rate. The Coupes will therefore be more difficult to find and more expensive when you do find one.

Some Volvo purists cast a jaundiced eye upon the Coupe, criticizing its "Chrysler" leather interior and the vinyl top as effete and non-Volvo. Expect the Coupes to retain value well, however, as the limited production keeps supply lower than demand.

Note, too, that the 262C/Coupes use the PRV V-6 that is so disdained in the 264, and has exactly the same problems. You can replace the camshafts via the passenger compartment, replace the entire engine, or put in a V-8—it will fit here too—but the latter option will have a negative impact on the car's value in the long run, destroying the car's authenticity.

The 262C/Coupe doesn't seem to suffer rust any more than any contemporary Volvo, Bertone doing as good a job on the body as

The last year of the 262 based Coupes was 1981, distinguished by the small chin spoiler. *Volvo*

the Swedish factory. Nor are there any unusual problems associated with the vinyl top, although cars left out in the elements or abused will see normal deterioration of the roof fabric.

As a limited production exotic, the 262C/Coupe is benign from a maintenance and upkeep standpoint, with the exception of the V-6 engine. Living with one shouldn't present any more problem than its six-cylindered sibling, the 264. But watch that roofline. Also, make sure that you fit in the car if you plan to drive your Coupe!

83

700 Series 1982-1992

The Same, Only Different

"New from its 10-spoke alloy wheels up" is how the then Volvo of America Corporation described the new 1983 Volvo 760GLE as it was introduced to the US market. That wasn't entirely true. On sale in Europe since February 1982, the 760GLE had a few carry-over items from the 260 Series it superseded, most notably in the drivetrain, but it nevertheless was a significantly different automobile.

The body was entirely new, although unmistakably a Volvo. It was larger inside and looked larger than—though dimensionally very close to—the 240 Series. A longer wheelbase than the 240/260 Series increased rear seat room, thanks to less encroachment by the rear wheel arches, and the high tail maintained the large trunk. And though its razor-crease corners didn't look it, the 760, with wedge-shaped front end and high rear deck, was significantly more aerodynamic than its predecessors and the equal of other sedans then available, regardless of how rounded. (That the drag coefficient was just under 0.40 shows how far we've come since then.)

MacPherson struts were retained for the front suspension, but a new live-axle arrangement was designed for the rear. Via longitudinal links above and below the differential, a wishbone subframe transferred acceleration and braking forces to the chassis, isolating the body from noise and vibration. Trailing links located the axle fore and aft, a Panhard rod provided lateral location, while coil springs carried vertical loads, along with gas-filled shocks. Volvo claimed most of the benefits of independent rear suspension with significantly less cost and maintenance.

Two engines were offered in the 760GLE in the United States for 1983. The B28F V-6 was carried over from the 260 Series but coupled to a new-for-Volvo four-speed overdrive automatic transmission, designated AW71. "More exotic," per Volvo, was the 2.4 liter VW-produced diesel inline six, though turbocharged for 103bhp. That engine was available only with the M46 four-speed manual transmission, with electrically operated

Volvo called the 1983 760GLE "new from the wheels up," even though it shared many components with earlier Volvos. Body, however, was all-new; French V-6 was carried over from 240 based GLE. *Volvo*

This is what Volvo means by Constant Track Rear Suspension, basically a well-located and isolated live axle. *Volvo*

1982 760GLE	
Dimensions	
Wheelbase	109.1in
Track	57.5/57.5in
Length	188.4in
Width	68.9in
Height	55.5in
Weight	3,130lb
Engine	
Type	Sohc V-6
Bore & stroke	3.58x2.87in (91x73mm)
Displacement	163ci (2849cc)
Compression	8.8:1
Fuel delivery	Bosch K-Jetronic injection
Horsepower	130bhp @ 5500rpm
Torque	153lb-ft @ 2750rpm
Chassis and Drivetrain	
Layout, engine/drivetrain	F/R
Frame/body	Unit steel
Transmission	Four-speed automatic
Rear axle ratio	3.54:1
Suspension, F/R	Strut/live axle
Tires	195/60R-15
Brakes	Disc/disc
Performance	
0-60mph	11.4sec
1/4 mile	18.3sec @ 76mph
Fuel mileage	17mpg
Top speed	N/A

overdrive available previously and elsewhere from Volvo.

As the flagship of the Volvo line, the 760GLE was rife with standard luxury features, including sunroof, automatic climate control, cruise control, heated driver's and passenger's seats, foglamps, central locking, and power windows and outside mirrors.

At around $20,000, depending on engine and upholstery chosen (leather was optional), this was the farthest Swedish salient into luxury territory yet. Yet *Road & Track* called the 760GLE "a sound, stylish, carefully planned example of the current state of the automotive art, and that it is perfectly ready to lead Volvo's step up in class."

1984

Volvo followed up a successful year with the 760GLE with refinements and more power. In response to customer demand, an

Molded cockpit dash of the 1983 760GLE was a long way from even the 164 dash of ten years before. *Volvo*

Seats in the 760GLE looked more like a Scandinavian modern furniture showroom than an automotive interior. *Volvo*

Volvo turbocharged Volkswagen's diesel for 1983 and put it in the 760GLE with the M46 manual transmission. However, in 1985, the turbodiesel was available only with an automatic. *Volvo*

The 740 Turbo with its skin on. Turbo was identified by the black grille with Turbo script. *Volvo*

automatic became available with the turbo-diesel (TD), this the ZF22L four-speed with lockup torque converter.

The 157hp turbocharged B23FT four-cylinder arrived in late springtime, though with 0–60mph times in the eight-second area. Owners would have little excuse for being late for anything. The model, naturally, was called the 760 Turbo.

The 740GLE combined the luxury of the 760 with a more economical 2.3 liter four, in either 114hp or turbo 160hp versions. *Volvo*

1985

In 1985, the 700 Series grew yet again. Two new models joined the line-up in the fall, the 750GLE and 740 Turbo. As the nomenclature suggests, these models were four-cylinder variants of the 760 line (never mind that, with the same engine, the 760 Turbo is too).

The fours, however, were part of the new B230 family of low-friction engines introduced in turbocharged form the year before. The turbocharged B230FT was rated at 160hp at 5300rpm, while the naturally aspirated B230F produced 114hp at 5400rpm. The B21FT continued only on the 240-based Turbo model.

A wagon version of the 740GLE was introduced in mid-year 1985.

The 740GLE had most of the amenities of the 760GLE (minus automatic climate control, for example, except with air conditioning and heated driver's seat standard) but with a smaller, less-powerful and more-economical engine, which could be had with manual or automatic transmission. The 740GLE also had 14in wheels rather than the 15in rims on the 760 and 740 Turbo. The 740 Turbo also stood out from the GLE with a black grille and trim. The 760 Turbo continued in 1985, sharing all the luxury touches of the 760GLE and 760TD. New aero-styled alloy wheels distinguished the 760 line, and the external mirrors were heated. The turbodiesels, incidentally, were produced through the end of the calendar year as 1984 models.

1985 740 Turbowagon	
Dimensions	
Wheelbase	109.1in
Track	57.9/57.5in
Length	188.4in
Width	69.3in
Height	56.5in
Weight	3,115lb
Engine	
Type	Sohc I-4
Bore & stroke	3.78x3.15in (96x80mm)
Displacement	141ci (2316cc)
Compression	8.7:1
Fuel delivery	Bosch LH-Jetronic injection
Horsepower	160bhp @ 5300rpm
Torque	187lb-ft @ 2900rpm
Chassis and Drivetrain	
Layout, engine/drivetrain	F/R
Frame/body	Unit steel
Transmission	Four-speed manual plus overdrive
Rear axle ratio	3.54:1
Suspension, F/R	Strut/live axle
Tires	195/60R-15
Brakes	Disc/disc
Performance	
0-60mph	8.4sec
1/4 mile	16.6sec @ 85.5mph
Fuel mileage	24mpg
Top speed	115mph (est.)

1986

The Turbo version of the 700 Series wagon finally joined the Volvo line-up in 1986. Otherwise, detail changes dominated the series for 1986.

A new black egg-crate grille, model-specific wheels, and new seats with more lateral support and new velour and leather

Introduced in February of 1985, the 740GLE Wagon was the yuppies' choice for antique hauling. The illustrated 1986 model was available with 2.3 liter gas or 2.4 liter turbodiesel. *Volvo*

The 760GLE Turbo defied Volvo's numerical designation system with the turbocharged four-cylinder engine. *Volvo*

Low-friction B230F four-cylinder engine, here in the spacious 740GLE engine compartment, was intro- duced in 1986. A turbocharged version was also available. *Volvo*

upholstery differentiated the 1986 Volvo 740 Turbo, along with new badge typeface. The 740GLE got new badging, two-speed seat heaters, and the availability of the D24T engine. The 760GLE got the two-speed bun warmers too, along with a power adjustable driver's seat and electrically heated, color-keyed power remote control mirrors.

Volvo went for an air bag with the 1987 760, as well as restyling the model's dash. *Volvo*

1987

Falling demand for diesels led to the demise of Herr Doktor's device from Volvo's American offerings. The turbodiesel had been offered in the 740 for one year, in the 760 for four.

The big news for the year, however, was the debut of the Volvo 780, a luxury coupe returning to the car maker's line, absent since the departure of the 262C/Coupe. The two-door was based on the 760 and like its predecessor, was designed and produced by Bertone in Italy. Available only with the V-6, the 780 was the plushest Volvo yet and more comfortable than the previous coupe, thanks to Bertone's restraint in the roofline department the second time around.

1988

Changes were so numerous for the 760—more than 2,000, said Volvo—that the company called it "same badge, new car." Body, suspension, and interior were all modified.

Most outwardly obvious of the changes to the 760 was new front-end styling, including large Euro-style headlamps. More subtle was the lowering and gentle rounding of the hood. Front and rear valances were also revised and there were new cast-alloy wheels specific to the 760.

Less obvious but perhaps more significant was the new Multi-link independent rear suspension that not only improved ride but also directional control on rough roads. Wagons didn't share the independent rear suspension, however; the live axle was retained for its greater carrying capacity. Bosch-designed ABS II antilock braking was new and standard on all 760s (as well as the 780 Coupe, 740 Turbo models, and optional on the 760GLE).

A new dashboard in the 760 combined classic white-on-black dials and improved ergonomics. Controls for the new Electronic Climate Control package shared the center console with Volvo's System 7145 sound system, an excellent but complex unit with more buttons than most calculators. Air bags were made standard on all 760 series models and 740 Turbos, and could be optioned on 740s not already so equipped.

All 760 wagons and most sedans were powered by the 2.3 liter turbo four. The 2.8 liter V-6 was also available and the only choice in the limited-volume 780. The 780 received the mechanical upgrades of the 760 Series, including the independent rear suspension and the new climate control system.

In addition to the changes already mentioned, a power-operated sunroof and power mirrors became standard on all 740 models.

A new front end went on the 1988 760GLE, available with V-6 or turbo four engines. *Volvo*

1989

The 1989 model year saw the 700 Series bracketed by new models on the top and bottom of the line, and two new engines were added to the menu at Chez Volvo 700. The new models were the 740GL (the 740 of 1988 grew a suffix for 1989), available in sedan and wagon versions. The other was the 780 Turbo, coupe buyers getting the choice of the turbo four in addition to the naturally aspirated V-6.

The two new engines included the B230FT+, what Volvo called "a further development" of the turbo four. Reprogrammed electronic boost controls raised peak power to 175hp at 5300rpm, with maximum torque

Multi-link independent rear suspension went under the 760 in 1988. *Volvo*

Volvo reprised the 262C with the 780 Coupe debuting in 1988. Like the earlier coupe, it had a body by Bertone as well. *Volvo*

Ghost drawing shows twin cams and counter-rotating balance shaft of the new-for-1989 sixteen-valve B234F engine. *Volvo*

remaining at 187lb-ft at 2900rpm. The engine was available only in the 780 Turbo.

Volvo joined the multi-valve club with the B234F. Though similar in dimensions, the four-valve-per-cylinder engine had a new block that accommodated a pair of balance shafts, which smoothed the vibrations (secondary or rocking forces) typical of four-cylinder engines. The head, of course, was all new, with double overhead cams operating the valves via self-adjusting hydraulic tappets. Both the cams and balance shafts were driven by toothed belts. The 2.3 liter engine was rated at an impressive 153bhp at 5700rpm, 150lb-ft of torque at a relatively high 4450rpm.

The 740GLE was the sole recipient of the B234F engine in the 1989 model year and for North America only after January 1, 1989. Available in either four-door sedan or five-door wagon and with either four-speed manual plus overdrive or four-speed automatic, even Volvo admitted "For those who enjoy running through the gears on a twisting mountain road, the manual is the obvious choice." For those who chose the automatic, it was the AW72L four-speed with lockup torque converter.

The 740GL still used the eight-valve B230F, but went up in wheel size from the 740 to 15in steel wheels with aero-style wheel covers. All 740s—all Volvos for that matter—

came standard with audio packages. All 740s included factory-installed 4x20in high-output power amplifier and 150mm coaxial front door speakers standard. The 740GLE for 1989 had new aero-style alloy wheels and could be distinguished from 1988 GLEs by the 16 Valve badge on its tail.

The 740 Turbo received only detail changes for 1989, as did the 760 line. The 780, as noted, added the Turbo variant which was only available with the four-speed automatic but also had Multi X spoke-style alloy wheels to set it apart from lesser 780s.

1990

A styling update graced all 740s for the 1990 model year, while an even hotter Generation 3 turbo motor filled the engine compartment of the 740 Turbo and the 760 wagon (optional in the 760 sedan). Choosing the 780 Turbo meant an even hotter version of the turbo four called the Turbo +.

The restyle of the 740 involved a lower and more steeply raked grille, large European-style halogen headlamps, and sleeker integration of the front bumper and spoiler,

The rare (and expensive) 780 Turbo of 1989 featured a 175hp turbo four, the extra output a product of the Turbo + electronic boost control. The model was distinguished from ordinary V-6 powered Coupes by the Multi X alloy wheels. *Volvo*

as well as a taillamp assembly similar to that of the 780 Coupe.

The nomenclature was reshuffled again, with 740 (no suffix) again becoming the base model, while the 740GL was the upgrade and

1989 740 Turbo	
Dimensions	
Wheelbase	109.1in
Track	57.9/57.5in
Length	188.4in
Width	69.3in
Height	55.5in
Weight	3,009lb
Engine	
Type	Sohc I-4
Bore & stroke	3.78x3.15in. (96x80mm)
Displacement	141ci (2316cc)
Compression	8.7:1
Fuel delivery	LH Lambda Sond
Horsepower	160bhp @ 5300rpm
Torque	187lb-ft @ 2900rpm
Chassis and Drivetrain	
Layout, engine/drivetrain	F/R
Frame/body	Unit steel
Transmission	Four-speed manual plus overdrive
Rear axle ratio	3.54:1
Suspension, F/R	Strut/live axle
Tires	195/65R15
Brakes	Disc/disc
Performance	
0-60mph	7.8sec
1/4 mile	16sec @ 86.5mph
Fuel mileage	20–25mpg (EPA)
Top speed	N/A

1989 740GLE	
Dimensions	
Wheelbase	109.1in
Track	57.9/57.5in
Length	188.4in
Width	69.3in
Height	55.5in
Weight	3,015lb
Engine	
Type	Dohc I-4, four valves per cylinder
Bore & stroke	3.78x3.15in (96x80mm)
Displacement	141ci (2316cc)
Compression	10.1:1
Fuel delivery	LH Lambda Sond
Horsepower	153bhp @ 5700rpm
Torque	150lb-ft @ 4450rpm
Chassis and Drivetrain	
Layout, engine/drivetrain	F/R
Frame/body	Unit steel
Transmission	Four-speed automatic
Rear axle ratio	4.10:1
Suspension, F/R	Strut/live axle
Tires	185/65HR-15
Brakes	Disc/disc
Performance	
0-60mph	9.6sec
1/4 mile	17.2sec @ 82mph
Fuel mileage	18–24mpg (EPA)
Top speed	125mph (est.)

the 740GLE the top of the line, the 740 Turbo holding down the sports model job again. From the rear, badges differentiated the various 740 models, while from the front the 740 and 740GL could be identified by a black vertical-bar grille, the 740GLE by a chromed vertical-bar grille, and the 740 Turbo by its black egg-crate grille.

From the side, the Turbo stood out with 16in "swept" five-spoke alloy wheels and 205/55R16V Michelin MXV2 tires. The 740 and 740GL had black-painted steel wheels with full wheel covers, the 740GLE ten-spoke aero-style alloy wheels. The sixteen-valve GLE was largely unchanged for 1990, while the 740 differed from the 740GL in that it was not available with a sunroof (standard on the GL, power optional) and its visor vanity mirror was not illuminated and cost about $350 less.

The Generation 3 version of the B230FT in the 740 Turbo had more horsepower and torque than the B23FT of 1989, but even more important were drivability improvements. A smaller turbine in the turbocharger, a more efficient exhaust manifold, and recalibration of the fuel injection and ignition increased

peak power to 162bhp at 4800rpm and torque to 195lb-ft at 3450, but with peak boost coming in at 1800rpm, there's less turbo lag and accompanying lunge as the boost makes its belated appearance. Optional from Volvo was a Turbo+ kit that hiked output to 188bhp at 5100rpm and torque to 206lb-ft at 2900rpm, available on new 740 Turbos equipped with manual transmissions.

The 760GLE V-6 was unchanged, while the 760 Turbo had the Generation 3 version of the B230FT with an automatic transmission.

The 780 Coupe V-6 got the Multi-X alloy wheels of the 1989 780 Turbo, new releases for the front seatbacks for easier entry and exit from the rear seats, and a new grille with vertical chrome bars to differentiate it from the 780 Turbo's black egg-crate design. The 780 Turbo received the 188bhp Turbo+ version of the B230FT Generation 3 engine as standard equipment; the four-speed automatic was still the only transmission choice.

1991

The 700 Series was partially eclipsed by the new 900 Series introduced in 1991. The 760 Series disappeared in its entirety and the

Only fifty special 740 Turbo sedans were built in 1990 as New York Show Specials, essentially a standard model with monochromatic paint and a styling kit that included a wing on the rear deck. *Volvo*

780 was simply renamed Coupe for what was announced in advance as its final year. The V-6 version of the 780 was dropped, and all Coupes were powered by the 188hp turbo four. The front antiroll bar was increased in diameter and a rear bar was added for the first time. A compact disc changer and antitheft circuitry were added to the stereo circuitry. Volvo set production at "less than 400," and anticipating future collector status, applied a plaque with the signature of Nuccio Bertone to the dashboard of every 1991 Coupe.

The 740 line was simplified to 740 and 740 Turbo. Sunroof cars were no longer identified as a GL and the 740 was available with the eight-valve engine and an automatic transmission only. The 740 Turbo was powered by the 162hp turbo four and had the choice of the M46 manual four-speed plus overdrive or the AW71 four-speed automatic. Both 740 and 740 Turbo came in four- and five-door versions. The 740GLE was another casualty of the 900 Series.

1992

The 700 Series line continued unchanged in terms of models and engines; however, along with the 900 Series cars, the 700 Series chassis was redesigned to resist penetration in side collisions and absorb the energy of the impact throughout the body.

The standard 1990 740 Turbo had aero headlamps, egg-crate grille, and fan-blade wheels. *Volvo*

Called Side Impact Protection System (SIPS), it's basically a reengineering and strengthening of the B-pillar and floor pan to redirect the crash forces throughout the car.

In addition to SIPS, antilock brakes (ABS) went on all 700 Series cars in 1992. Other new features across the board for the 700 Series are pyrotechnic seatbelt pretensioners, an integral padded headrest for the front seats, an automatic locking differential for improved traction, power remote-control outside mirrors, and a more powerful battery and alternator. Manual transmissions, however, dropped from the option list for all 700 Series models.

The 1990 740GLE featured a grille with bright vertical bars and flush alloy wheels. *Volvo*

Volvo 740 and 740GL also got the new grille and headlamps in 1990. *Volvo*

Visit Stockholm and you'll see stretched 740 limos lined up in front of the better hotels, though chauffeurs consider Cadillac limos "the real thing."

He who dies with the most Volvos wins? Only if one of them is a 740 hearse like this one from Trollhattan, Sweden, with big glass windows to show off your fancy casket.

This would be the final iteration for the 700 Series, however; the model was dropped in anticipation of the 850. Production tapered off during the year.

What to Look For

The 700 Series has not yet reached collector status, but some 700s make better living companions than others. The V-6 engine tends to be as much of a problem in the 700 Series as it was in the 260 Series. Poorly designed lubrication systems result in worn camshafts and the need to replace them or the engine. Volvo sells a kit, complete with hole saw and rubber plugs, to remove camshafts from the passenger compartment through the firewall.

Replacement PRV V-6 engines are available and some owners have installed Chevrolet or Ford engines in the engine bay. They fit with no problem and the proper setup will send Camaro owners back to their dealerships muttering about "slower than a Volvo."

The PRV V-6 was improved over its tour at Volvo, and the last several years were much better than the early years. But there's little reason to seek out the V-6 over the various four-cylinder models, turbo or not, considering the potential cost. As one observer noted, "You'll buy a camshaft and then a camshaft and then a new engine."

The VW-built diesel engine was available only in turbocharged form on the 700 Series. If hanging out with Peterbilt drivers is your idea of fun, the turbodiesels (through 1986)

offer reasonable performance, though Peterbilt drivers will be the only ones you'll be able to outrun at the stoplight grand prix.

Of course, if you want to remain all-Volvo, stay with the four-cylinder engines, especially the turbocharged ones. Intercooling, as of 1984, substantially increased horsepower. A retrofit of the intercooler is available for turbocharged Volvos not so equipped.

Also be aware that while the Aisin-Warner automatic transmissions, and the Volvo manual transmission, are known for being bulletproof, the ZF automatics don't share that reputation. The ZF was used primarily with naturally aspirated 740s (check the chart in the appendices for specific applications). The ZF will reveal impending failure by creeping when the engine is revved with the transmission in neutral, with the engine and transmission completely warmed. The turbodiesels with the ZF automatic . . . how many reasons do you need to look elsewhere?

A low-mileage Volvo 740 with the five-speed is a good bet for an everyday driver. There's lots of troublefree driving at a reasonable price, especially after someone else takes that first shot of depreciation. Add the turbo and you've got an extra dash of excitement. Add aftermarket antiroll bars (standard issue caters more to the general market than the enthusiast) and you'll have people wondering why that Volvo driver—you—is smiling so much. And you can drive that smile all the way to the bank.

Chapter 10

★   **940**
★   **960**

900 Series 1991-Current

A New Leader For A New Decade

The king is dead, long live the king. Volvo discarded the 760 Series and decimated the ranks of the 740 in 1991, but it was in favor of the new 900 Series.

The new cars were strongly reminiscent of the old 700s, and casual observers would have trouble picking the two lines apart. But there were definite differences in the grille, and a more steeply slanted rear window with a much smoother treatment of the C-pillar makes the 900 Series easy to tell from its forefather. The new face for the 900 Series had the traditional Volvo grille in a raked position, flanked by integrated foglights and large European-style halogen headlamps.

1991

For 1991, the 900 Series was comprised of three different 940s, each available in four-door sedan or five-door wagon versions. The basic model is the 940GLE, if a car with a list price of $27,885 can be called basic. Power for this model comes from the sixteen-valve 2.3 liter B234F four-cylinder coupled to a standard four-speed automatic transmission. The standard equipment list was long, including air conditioning, power steering, power-assisted four-wheel brakes, power sunroof, and audio system.

The 940SE included the more powerful B230FT as the standard powerplant, and

The 960 corrected one of the biggest shortcomings of the 700 Series, the awkward and angular C-pillar.

New swept-spoke wheels and trunk-mounted badge identify the new 1991 model. *Volvo*

The biggest news of the 960 was under the hood, the B6304F inline six-cylinder engine. Its 3.0 liters and twenty-four valves produced 201hp, a high for Volvo. *Volvo*

The 940GL sedan introduced in 1992 was the volume leader, featuring the naturally aspirated 2.3 liter four-cylinder engine and Volvo's constant-track live rear axle. *Volvo*

raised the luxury quotient by including automatic climate control, eight-way power adjustable seats, and a six-speaker radio and cassette system. The 940 Turbo uses the same engine but is accessorized like the GLE and chassis-tuned for more sporty handling. The only transmission for either model, however, is the four-speed automatic.

1992

The absence of a six-cylinder engine in Volvo's flagship line lasted exactly one year. The introduction of the 1992 Volvo 960 brought it back. But it wasn't the PRV V-6 that had been around since the mid-seventies, rather a completely new inline six designed and produced by Volvo. Despite the seem-

1991 940 Turbo	
Dimensions	
Wheelbase	109.1in
Track	57.9/57.5in
Length	191.7in
Width	69.3in
Height	55.5in
Weight	3,065lb
Engine	
Type	Sohc I-4
Bore & stroke	96x80mm
Displacement	141ci (2316cc)
Compression	8.7:1
Fuel delivery	LH Lambda Sond
Horsepower	162bhp @ 4800rpm
Torque	195lb-ft @ 3450rpm
Chassis and Drivetrain	
Layout, engine/drivetrain	F/R
Frame/body	Unit steel
Transmission	Four-speed automatic
Rear axle ratio	3.73:1
Suspension, F/R	Strut/live axle
Tires	205/55R16
Brakes	Disc/disc, ABS
Performance	
0-60mph	8.9sec
1/4 mile	16.8sec @ 81.8mph
Fuel mileage	20–25mpg (EPA)
Top speed	N/A

1991 960	
Dimensions	
Wheelbase	109.1in
Track	57.9/59.8in
Length	191.7in
Width	69.3in
Height	55.5in
Weight	3,515lb
Engine	
Type	Dohc I-6, four valves per cylinder
Bore & stroke	3.27x3.54in (83x90mm)
Displacement	178ci (2922cc)
Compression	10.7:1
Fuel delivery	Bosch Motronic injection
Horsepower	201bhp @ 6000rpm
Torque	197lb-ft @ 4300rpm
Chassis and Drivetrain	
Layout, engine/drivetrain	F/R
Frame/body	Unit steel
Transmission	Four-speed automatic
Rear axle ratio	3.31:1
Suspension, F/R	Struts/independent
Tires	195/65VR-15
Brakes	Disc/disc, ABS
Performance	
0-60mph	10.1sec
1/4 mile	17.4sec @ 82.5mph
Fuel mileage	18–25mpg (EPA)
Top speed	135mph (est.)

The 1992 940 Turbo had a 162hp turbo four and four-speed automatic transmission, and was available in sedan or wagon bodies. Black egg-crate grille and fan-blade wheels differentiate the Turbo from nonturbo 940s. *Volvo*

ingly out-of-fashion configuration—new six-in-a-row engines are rare—the new B6304F is as technologically advanced as any engine on the market, and more so than most.

The 960 itself shares outward appearances with the 940, although both models received significant reengineering of internal body structure that provided increased safety in side collisions. The design, dubbed Side Impact Protection System (SIPS), controls the forces in a lateral impact, directing them into the floor and via a stronger B-pillar, into the roof, decreasing the penetration of a colliding vehicle.

The 3.0 liter B6304F engine is only 4in longer than the company's 2.3 liter four and light, thanks to finite element analysis and all-aluminum-alloy construction. Cylinders have cast-in iron liners, and cast-iron reinforcements are used in the main bearing caps, which are cast into a single lower crankcase. Volvo describes the engine as built like a layer cake—from the top, the camshaft housing, cylinder head, cylinder block, lower crankcase, and oil pump, all bolting together

without traditional gaskets. Liquid gaskets instead ensure close tolerances.

The double-overhead-camshaft head has pent-roof combustion chambers that by careful design require only regular unleaded fuel

The exterior of the 1993 960 was unchanged, but this interior look shows a dash with a passenger-side air bag and a large-format sound system.

The 1993 940 and 960 wagons had a 60/40 split rear seat with headrests that automatically retract when the seatback is lowered and three-point belt for the center passenger, possibly a world's first. Photo shows the child seat integrated into the center armrest.

despite a 10.7:1 compression ratio. The twin camshafts are driven by a toothed belt and open the twenty-four valves via hydraulic tappets.

The Bosch Motronic 1.8 electronic engine management system controls both fuel injection and ignition. There is no conventional distributor; six coils attach directly to each spark plug.

The engine is rated at 201bhp at 6000rpm, the most ever from a Volvo automotive engine, with torque at 171lb-ft at 4300rpm. The only transmission choice is an electronically controlled four-speed overdrive automatic, the AW40. Calculating gear choice requirements from various inputs, the transmission is also controlled by the driver's mode selection switch: economy, sport (which delays upshifts for increased performance), and winter, which blocks out first and second to minimize wheelspin on slippery surfaces. There's even a down-slope mode which gears down automatically on downhills to provide engine braking.

The 940GL became the base model for 1992, replacing the 940GLE of 1991 and losing the sixteen-valve four-cylinder in the process. The GL is powered by the B230F four producing 114bhp at 5400 rpm. The 940 Turbo was reprised for 1992 basically unchanged.

All 900 Series cars for 1992 were available in four-door sedan or five-door wagon versions.

1993

The 900 Series finally swallowed the 700s whole. There had been a lot of overlap between the 740 and 940, sharing the basic engine and chassis, and with the arrival of the 850 GLT, Volvo decided to simplify its line. The 940 line would include for 1993 naturally aspirated and turbocharged four-cylinder engines in a four-door or five-door chassis and a choice of three trim levels, rather inelegantly named "Base," "Option Package 1," and "Option Package 2."

Base included all-season radials, automatic transmission and automatic locking

The 1993 940 wagon with the Option Package 1 came equipped with twenty-spoke alloy wheels, a power sunroof, leather-faced upholstery, and a full-logic cassette deck. A roof rack was optional.

differential, power driver's seat, windows and mirrors, cruise control, and heated front seats. Option Package 1 added alloy wheels, power sunroof, leather upholstery, and full logic cassette. Option Package 2 replaced the standard 114hp engine with the perennial 164hp turbocharged four, while adding an egg-crate grille, front foglights, color-keyed bumpers (when metallic paint was specified), 195/65-15 H-rated tires, and a badge that says 940 Turbo on the trunklid. All 940 models had fuel tanks increased from 15.8 to 19.8 gallons, and nonturbo models got lock-up torque converters.

For the 960 line, the sedans continued virtually unchanged, upgrades restricted to the wagon. Even there it was just a bigger fuel tank, up to 19.8 gallons, and added safety for the center rear seating position in the form of a headrest and three-point belt.

What to Look For

The 900 Series cars are still new cars as this is written and the new inline six series engines and the electronically controlled transmission too new to show a reliability track record yet. The 960s, however, are elegant automobiles and have been favorably received by the press.

The 940s continue to embody proven technology. Styling is notably improved over the 700 Series, particularly the smoothing of the awkward C-pillar of that Series. Despite the luxurious trappings and automatic everything, Volvos still come with odometers that read up to 999,999 miles and are still capable of delivering. The 900 Series cars should provide years of safe and reliable motoring in the best of Volvo tradition.

★	**66**
★★	**343, 345**
★★★	**360**
★★★¹/₂	**360 GLT**

66 and 300 Series 1975-1991

Dutch Treat

The United States has been an inspiration for Volvo and a more than welcome market, yet one series of Volvos has never been available in the United States. And short of going to Europe, you won't get to drive one of the "small Volvos." Not that Volvo wouldn't like to have a wider range in America, and at one time was poised to enter the small-car market in the United States. But changes in the exchange rate ended those plans and because they haven't been certified for sale in the United States, the small Volvo is a rare if not nonexistent sight on this side of the Atlantic.

The saga of the small Volvo began in 1973 when Volvo bought a one-third share in DAF, a Dutch company that since the early sixties

The DAF design was given Volvo styling cues and badges when it went into production as the Volvo. *Volvo*

had been building small and somewhat idiosyncratic vehicles around a unique (at least for automobiles) rubber-belt-and-pulley continuously variable transmission (CVT), which DAF called Variomatic. With the development of the 140 Series taxing the relatively small Swedish firm's technical and financial capabilities, adding the little DAF to the Volvo line-up seemed a quick way to get into the market. By January 1975, Volvo owned 75 percent of the Dutch company, changing its name to Volvo Car BV in May of that year.

Volvo initially only assumed responsibility for marketing the DAFs in Scandinavia. The new DAF 66 featured a de Dion rear axle, an advanced Variomatic, and an 1108cc Renault engine. And although it was much improved over earlier DAFs, it was not until 1975 that Volvo was convinced that the model was sufficiently improved to put a Volvo-looking front end, complete with diagonal bar, and its own name on it, calling it the Volvo 66.

The Volvo badge on the steering wheel can't alter the minimalist interior—though three-point belts were provided for rear seat passengers as well as those in the front. *Volvo*

A 1289cc Renault engine was used in both two-door and hatchback versions. A Volvo 66GL, with fancier trim and features, was introduced to the Swedish market in

The Volvo 66 looked like a DAF from any angle—but why is this one in the passing lane? *Volvo*

The Volvo 66 was powered by a 1300cc Renault inline four with rear-mounted CVT transmission. Underhood storage of spare wheel and jack was typical continental economy car practice.

1976 343	
Dimensions	
Wheelbase	94.3in
Track	53.1/54.3in
Length	161in
Width	65.4in
Height	54.9in
Weight	2,160lb
Engine	
Type	Ohv I-4
Bore & stroke	2.99x3.03in (76x77mm)
Displacement	85.2ci (1397cc)
Compression	9.5:1
Fuel delivery	One Solex (1V)
Horsepower	70bhp @ 5500rpm
Torque	80lb-ft @ 3500rpm
Chassis and Drivetrain	
Layout, engine/drivetrain	F/R
Frame/body	Unit steel
Transmission	CVT
Rear axle ratio	3.84–14.20:1
Suspension, F/R	Strut/De Dion
Tires	155SR-13 or 175/70SR-13
Brakes	Disc/drum
Performance	
0-60mph	15.4sec
1/4 mile	N/A
Fuel mileage	21–26mpg
Top speed	N/A

1976. The hatchback version was sold only through 1977, though the two-door Volvo 66 continued through 1981.

1976 and the 343

The Volvo 343 was introduced in 1976, coming on the Swedish market in September. Development of this model had been initiated by DAF to be the successor of the 66—originally to be called the DAF 77—and therefore used the Variomatic transmission with a Renault 1397cc inline four in the same front-engine, rear-drive configuration. The front end of the 343 bore a strong resemblance to that of the 240 Series Volvos, but the new model was roundly criticized for poor quality—rattles, leaks, and underdevelopment—as well as being underpowered, underheated, and, with the Variomatic, peculiar in the way its power got to the ground. It was all very un-Volvolike.

1978–1979

Volvo attacked these shortcomings directly, with a stringent quality control program, "rally" kits to enhance performance, and a multitude of detail improvements for the 1978 model year. A specially trimmed version was called The Black Beauty.

In 1979 came the biggest change, a manual transmission. This was simply the same transmission that was used in the 240 Series, but it eliminated the unusual operating characteristics of the Variomatic—and was 1,000 kroner cheaper as well. By 1982, only 15 percent of 343s would come with the belt-drive transmission.

The de Dion rear suspension, however, was retained, but the high rear floor pan, and resulting high rear seat, remained, an economically unalterable vestige of the rear-mounted CVT. Trim and fitments became more and more like a Volvo as well, even to having electrically heated seats on all but the most basic models.

1980

The trend continued in the 1980 model year. A five-door hatchback, the 345GL, was added to the line which included the 343L

The 343 still had the look of a generic European econobox, though the styling was sharpened with aero headlamps and a steeper slope to the rear window. GL version had Variomatic optional, but most buyers chose the manual gearbox.

(manual transmission only) or upmarket DL and GL (manual or Variomatic).

The small Renault engine was joined in model year 1981 with the 1986cc B19A Volvo engine, a smaller version of Volvo's overhead-cam B21, a virtual powerhouse making 95hp and tacking on an S to DL and GL models so equipped.

1982

The 1982 340 line was simplified and the front end redesigned to look even more like a Volvo. The 343L and 343/345DL came with the Renault engine, Variomatic optional on the DL. The 343/345GLS was powered by the Volvo-built B19A.

A pre-1982 343 (or 345) can be spotted by its grille, which looks attached to, rather than fitted in, the cars front end, as on this 343DL.

1983

A hot 360GLT, with 115bhp from its B19E engine, arrived in 1983. As the E in its designation suggests, the engine was fuel injected, and featured electronic ignition, an electric fuel pump, and a thermostatically controlled cooling fan. A new five-speed

The 343 hatchback was a big improvement over the combi styling of the 66.

Note the conventional trunk rather than hatchback on this 340DL.

Volvo dropped the 343/345 model designation in 1983, opting for 340 and 360, which designated trim level rather than number of doors. The 340 came with either carbureted 1.3 liter Renault or 1.9 liter Volvo engine.

transmission was also part of the package, as were external embellishments including alloy wheels, a rear spoiler, a front spoiler with driving lamps, and matte-black trim.

Also new was the 360GLS with 95hp carbureted B19A and a five-speed.

The 340 came in DL trim (with the Renault engine) or DL 2.0 liter (when equipped with the B19A), available either way with a four-speed or the Variomatic. Four hundred Autumn Specials, half in black and half in white, came with the French engine and five-cog transmission.

1984–1985

Two new four-door models were added to the 300 line-up in 1984, the 360GLS and 360GLE. Both came only with a five-speed manual and the 92bhp B19A or 116bhp B21E respectively, the latter with alloy rather than steel wheels. There was an even fancier

The 360 GLS designation means this five-door model has the 1.9 liter engine. Note the Volvo accessory wheels.

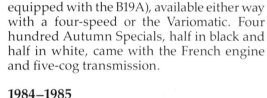

This 360 GLS five door has a factory sunroof.

360GLT, while the 340DL had its B14 Renault engine upgraded from 70 to 72bhp.

For 1985, the 300 Series received only minor changes, although a 54hp diesel was added for some export markets.

1986

A new engine option became available for the 1986 edition of the 340. This was a Renault-built 1.7 liter four making 82bhp and dubbed B172 in Volvospeak. Grille, bumpers, and rear lights were changed on all models, while a five-speed transmission became standard on all but the cheapest of the 300s. The Variomatic was still available, but down to 10 percent of the model range.

1987–1991

In 1987 the catalytic converter made its first appearance on the 300 Series, with all engines designed for high-octane unleaded fuel. Air conditioning became more widely available, previously limited to cars bound for (or built locally from completely knocked down—CKD—kits) tropical markets.

Minor changes, except for wider availability of emission controls, were the story

Lambda Sond badge on grille identifies this 360 GLS as a catalytic converter-equipped model built between 1987 and 1991.

for 1988. Or would have been, were it not for the millionth 300 Series car produced in March of that year. Despite the rocky start, the 300 Series had become a major component of the Volvo line in Europe. Production, however, was already being scaled back as the 460 came on stage. Changes were minor for the rest of its production, which ended on March 13, 1991.

From the start in 1976, 1,139,689 300 Series Volvos were produced. It may never have become a swan, but it was a pretty good showing for the ugly duckling from the Netherlands.

Volvo-like taillights, full wheel covers, and even pinstriping adorn this late-model two-door 360 GLS.

The 480 interior had remarkable back seat room for a sporty coupe. *Volvo*

the hatch was almost all glass and incorporated the wiper so needed on a car with this shape. The wedge front end broke with Volvo tradition, however, although marque identification was retained in the below-the-bumper grille opening that displayed the Volvo logo and diagonal bar.

The dash had a traditional analog tachometer and speedometer, white on black

1989 480 Turbo	
Dimensions	
Wheelbase	98.5in
Track	55.5in
Length	167.8in
Width	67.3in
Height	51.9in
Weight	2,288lb
Engine	
Type	Ohc I-4
Bore & stroke	3.19x3.29in (81.0x83.5mm)
Displacement	104.9ci (1721cc)
Compression	8.1:1
Fuel delivery	Bosch LH-Jetronic injection
Horsepower	120bhp @ 5400rpm
Torque	103lb-ft
Chassis and Drivetrain	
Layout, engine/drivetrain	F/F
Frame/body	Unit steel
Transmission	Five-speed manual
Final drive ratio	5.08:1
Suspension, F/R	Strut/beam
Tires	185/60HR-14
Brakes	Disc/disc, ABS
Performance	
0-60mph	9sec
1/4 mile	N/A
Fuel mileage	N/A
Top speed	124mph

with red dials, and an in-dash trip computer, with instantaneous and average fuel consumption and remaining range, as well as coolant, engine oil, and outside temperatures. Novelties included intermittent windshield wipers that went to continuous with full throttle, and activation of the rear wiper if the front wipers were on and reverse gear selected.

480ES Introduced

The 480ES, built at the same factory in the Netherlands that made the 300 Series Volvos, went on sale in Europe in 1986 and plans were to offer it in the United States beginning in autumn 1988 as a 1989 model. "We will be proud to have the 480 ES take its place next to the 240 Series and the 700 Series in the North American lineup," stated Joseph Nicolato, Volvo Cars of North America president, in a company press release.

But the dollar had been sinking, losing 32 percent of its value against the Dutch guilder between 1982 and 1988. Cost, instead of the $15,000 originally envisioned, would be closer to $20,000. The final nail in the coffin was Black Monday, October 18, 1987, when the New York Stock Exchange crashed. On February 8, 1988, Nicolato told US Volvo dealers that all import plans for the car were off. It was indeed that close.

More's the pity, because in early 1988 the 480 Turbo made its debut, though only on the European market. And if the 480ES had been desirable, the Turbo was truly lustworthy. Its B18FT engine produced 120bhp at 5400rpm and, important for drivability, torque peaked at 1800rpm instead of the 4600rpm of its naturally aspirated sibling, thanks to electronic boost control.

The model was outwardly distinguishable, in addition to its greater acceleration, by bumpers in body color instead of black, a larger front spoiler, and Turbo insignia on sides and rear. The dash, meanwhile, gained a turbo boost gauge, oil gauge, and voltmeter. Both Turbo and ES 480s received antilock braking, air conditioning, leather upholstery, and a sunroof for the 1988 model year.

For 1990, a major redesign of the naturally aspirated B18 engines meant that Volvo no longer had a fuel-injected engine with an unregulated catalytic converter. The electronic controls meant a slight increase in horsepower, a lowered torque peak for better drivability, and smoother idling. A central diagnostic system was added and, perhaps best of all, the engines no longer resembled Renault engines, according to a Volvo internal publication.

The Turbo was revised as well, with a new camshaft and modified boost for more power below 2000rpm and improved around-town performance. A four-speed automatic was also new for 1990. Changes were minimal for 1991.

480 Cabriolet

At the 1990 Geneva Motor Show, a design study based on the Volvo 480 was shown, a neat Paris Blue two-seater with a black convertible top. Essentially a 480 with the steel roof removed, the Cabrio had a padded "basket handle" roll bar and a fabric top that folded down beneath a hard tonneau made of "composite material." Special door panels would help retain occupants in case of a rollover accident.

Production start was considered for late 1990, but the decision was made not to build it. The 480 Cabrio became nothing more than a pretty design study.

The concept car that didn't make production was the 480 Cabriolet—on which safety-minded Swedes installed a roll bar. *Volvo*

440S

It shouldn't be surprising that a sedan version of the 480 was produced, only perhaps that the sports model came first. But indeed in June 1988 the Volvo 440 was shown to the press, with production starting the fall of that year as a 1989 model. The five-door hatchback was seen as overlapping the 200 and 300 ranges, both more than a little long in the tooth, and aimed squarely at a market already filled with the Ford Sierra, Mazda 626, Opel Ascona, Toyota Camry, and VW Passat, as well as the Swedish-built Saab 900. It was built on the same floor pan as the 480, and suspension, steering, and engine were virtually identical.

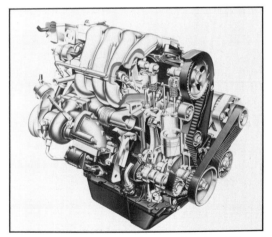

Cutaway of the turbo engine used in the 480 and 440 showed the single overhead cam and dished pistons of the Heron head design. *Volvo*

Volvo 440 was a four-door sedan variant of the 480 coupe. *Volvo*

Notchback styling of the 440GL concealed the hatchback flexibility. *Volvo*

Like its upscale siblings, the 440 came in different trim levels: base GL, GLT, and Turbo, the first two powered by the B18F, emission controlled (catalytic converter, oxygen sensor, and LH-Jetronic fuel injection), and producing 95bhp. The Turbo received the same 120bhp as the 480 Turbo (with similar smog equipment). The GL and GLT could do 0–60mph in about eleven seconds, the Turbo getting up to speed in about two seconds less. Volvo claimed fuel economy of around 35mpg in mixed driving.

Like the 440 Turbo, the GLT came with ABS and four-wheel disc brakes (though ABS was optional on the GL). Interiors were similar to the 480 in color and style, the trip computer available as an option on the GLT, standard on the Turbo. The two more expensive models also had alloy wheels, electrically adjustable and heated rearview mirrors, front-spoiler-mounted foglamps, and a small wing mounted on the notch of the hatch. The

Turbo was further distinguished from the GLT by a flat-black treatment of the grille.

460

With a growing preference in Europe for sedans over hatchbacks—sedans were perceived as more prestigious and, with a more sealed-off trunk area, actually are quieter on the road—Volvo spanned the gap between the 440 and 480 with the 460 in the 1990 model year. The grille and high rear deck imitated the new Volvo 940/960 Series cars, while the hood and long roofline link the 460 to the Volvo 440.

The 460 was available with the B18 engine in both naturally aspirated and turbo forms, and with five-speed manual or four-speed automatic transmissions.

US Importation?

Volvo Cars of North America, which so anticipated the 480ES, concedes now that the 400 Series will never reach these shores. The 800 Series, arriving in the United States as a 1993 model, further reduces any likelihood of official importation. And despite having been built with US safety specifications in mind and with emission-controlled engines available across the board, US laws effectively prohibit gray market importation.

To jump through all the bureaucratic hoops to get a 400 into the United States would be too expensive and time consuming, if at all possible, and you wouldn't be able to drive your 400 on the road legally even if you did.

The 440 Turbo had more horsepower, badges, five-spoke alloy wheels, and a rear wing to advertise it. *Volvo*

The 440 dash was similar to the 480's, illustrated by the 440GL dash shown. *Volvo*

850 1992-Current

The Newest Volvo

For small car companies, every new model is important. The success of the Volvo 850 is no less so for Volvo. With capacity worldwide exceeding demand, pundits have been calling for a shakeout of manufacturers and Volvo always seems to be mentioned in those discussions. With the 700 and 900 Series in upscale and further upscale positions, and the aging 240 in the more affordable range, the 850 is needed for the company to maintain an adequate spectrum of product to support its dealers as well as Volvo Cars of North America. And sales in North America

The Volvo 850 looked distinctly like a Volvo, as this 1992 European-spec car shows. *Volvo*

Ghost view of Volvo 850 clearly showed the transverse inline five-cylinder engine. *Volvo*

The transverse five is a snug fit under the 850 GLT's hood.

are critical to the survival of the parent company in Sweden.

That said, the Volvo 850 is a significant departure from traditional Volvo design. The 850 is front-drive, the first time a front-drive Volvo will be sold in the United States (the 480 and 440 as well as the earlier 343 were all front-drive but not sold in North America). Even more remarkable, a transverse in-line five-cylinder engine is being used in the 850. It's a snug fit, requiring an extremely compact five-speed manual transmission with three shafts. A four-speed automatic with torque-converter lockup is also being offered. Equal-length halfshafts minimize torque-sheer effects.

The engine, designated B5254F, is a modular version of the in-line six that's sited traditionally in the 960. As such, it's a twenty-valve (four valves per cylinder) design with a bore and stroke of 83 x 90mm. The naturally aspirated 2435cc engine is rated at 170hp.

The suspension is conventional at the front with MacPherson struts. However, at the rear is a Volvo-patented Delta-link semi-independent suspension. Delta-link is a sort of split-twisting-beam rear suspension, as popularized by the Volkswagen Golf/Rabbit, though with each side jointed near the elbows. Furthermore, double bushings allow the axle to oscillate around the pickup points, and gives a passive four-wheel-steering effect. This yields good turn-in with a stable cornering attitude through the turn. Most people will feel it as not feeling like a front-wheel-drive car. Antiroll bars are used front and rear. Brakes are disc front and rear, with three-channel ABS standard. Volvo mounts 195/60VR15 tires on 6.5 x 15in wheels.

Styling is obviously Volvo. In a parking lot of 700 and 900 Series cars, the 850 can go unnoticed. Yet its four-door shape is immediately identifiable as a Volvo, which should help it gain a foothold in the cut-throat competitive near-luxury market. Volvo's task will be getting the word out to prospective buyers in this segment.

Driving Impressions

Initial drives in US spec car gave impressions of a slightly smaller but by no means slow sedan. The five-cylinder motor makes noises similar to the Audi five-cylinder engines and loves to be revved right up to the redline. Attention has been paid to vibration and "bad" sounds, and it is evident. The 850's

1993 850 GLT	
Dimensions	
Wheelbase	104.9in
Track	59.8/57.9in
Length	183.5in
Width	69.3in
Height	55.1in
Weight	2,926lb
Engine	
Type	Dohc I-5, four valves per cylinder
Bore & stroke	3.27x3.54in (83x90mm)
Displacement	148.5ci (2435cc)
Compression	10.5:1
Fuel delivery	Bosch LH-Jetronic 3.2
Horsepower	170bhp @ 6000rpm
Torque	162lb-ft @ 3300rpm
Chassis and Drivetrain	
Layout, engine/drivetrain	F/F
Frame/body	Unit steel
Transmissions	Five-speed manual or four-speed automatic
Rear axle ratio	N/A
Suspension, F/R	Strut/semi-independent Delta-link
Tires	195/60VR15
Brakes	Disc/disc
Performance	
0-60mph	N/A
1/4 mile	N/A
Fuel mileage	N/A
Top speed	N/A

The interior shared the exterior's new-but-like-a-Volvo look; passenger side had glove box and air bag.

voice has that nice pear-shaped tone your vocal instructor always wanted.

Though the torque curve is broad, there's only so much you can do with 2.5 liters. Revs are needed to get the 850 to accelerate. The automatic shifted smoothly enough, but enthusiastic drivers will want the five speed which, along with the clutch, is light and easy to use. US cars get better sound-deadening material than their European counterparts, Americans preferring a quieter car. It works. At highway speeds, the loudest noise is the wind around the side mirrors—the clock is electronic.

The 850 should place Volvo in the thick of the near-luxury market with a price just under $25,000. But whether the front-drive 850 can steer customers away from the Acura dealerships remains to be seen.

Delta-link rear suspension resembles a twist-beam rear axle, but with a twist of its own.

Chapter 14

Volvos in Competition

"Volvo" and "competition" aren't words that are normally thought to go together, but the Volvo PV444, almost as soon as it was available, was in the hands of privateers, rallying and racing from California to Africa and just about every point in between. As often as not, they were successful, winning class and even overall victories. Never overpowered, Volvos have nonetheless shown enough speed to be competitive and more than enough stamina to finish. And finishing is the most basic prerequisite to winning.

Although there were some local efforts before World War II, the first major competition to see a Volvo entered was the 1949 Monte Carlo Rally, which had Hilding Ohlsson, Martin Carstedt, and Stig Cederholm competing in a PV444 with skis in a roof rack, probably one of the more unusual methods of roll protection ever. The team returned the following year to finish 12th overall.

A significant early result was in the 1956 Marathon de la Route where, of four PV444s entered, all finished, the best in 8th place. Less than half of their competitors completed the difficult event, which ran through France, Italy, and Yugoslavia.

About the same time, Americans were getting their first PV444s, Californians taking them to the track to win four straight sedan races. PV444s and PV544s dominated sedan racing on the East Coast as well, claiming the inaugural ten-hour Little Le Mans race at Lime Rock in 1957 and the first twelve-hour

The world's most famous PV544 must be the one brothers Jaswant and Joginder Singh drove to victory in the 1965 East Africa Safari Rally, here with the champions on the roof. The car was one of four work cars left by Volvo in Kenya after the 1964 Safari rally, reworked by the Singhs before the 1965 event. *John Switzer collection*

race at Marlboro in 1962. Through 1962, Volvos won four of the Lime Rock enduros.

European Rally Championships were won by PVs in 1958 and 1963 by Gunnar Andersson and in 1954 by Tom Trana. These factory-sponsored rally aces won many of the world's toughest rallies, although a privateer, driving a former team car won the strenuous East Africa Safari. This was Joginder Singh, who now has restored that very car to original condition.

Though heavy for a sports car, the P1800 won Class F-Production honors in the SCCA's initial American Road Race of Champions (ARRC) in 1964, driver Dick Hull repeating the performance at the third ARRC in 1966. In other SCCA action, Volvo won the Manufacturer's Rally Championship in 1968.

Parenthetically, the actual rally car is still owned by Joginder Singh, now in England, and restored—but to road rather than rally condition. *John Switzer collection*

The Safari Rally was no walk in the park, unless your park includes hog wallows. This was *on the* road. Imagine what it must have been like to go off! *John Switzer collection*

115

The Volvo Competition Service trademark was a two-fingered salute in a proper string-backed driving glove.

Richard Gordon chalks up Volvo's first professional US road-racing win in a ten-year-old Volvo. *Gary Gaska photo, courtesy iPd*

Volvo won the Group A European Touring Championship in 1985 with a team of two race-prepped 240 Turbos. Volvo Dealer Team Europe sponsored the entries run by team manager Rudi Eggenberger out of Switzerland, center. Drivers Sigfrid Müller,

Pierre Dieudonné, Thomas Lindström, and Gianfranco Brancatelli stand alongside one of the team cars. The team took five 1st places on their way to winning the season. *Volvo*

Richard Gordon, founder of Volvo competition parts supplier iPd Company, Inc., won the first professional road race for a Volvo in the United States with a win at Laguna Seca in a 142 in an IMSA Champion Spark Plug Challenge event. Gordon competed in both IMSA and SCCA events with the same 142, installing fiberglass fenders for SCCA races and steel for the IMSA meets. iPd, which still supplies performance parts for Volvos, is listed in the Sources section.

Volvo, under the auspices of Volvo Competition Services, sold Volvo speed parts in the mid-sixties and again in the mid-seventies. The inventory included suspension kits, carburetor/intake manifold setups, and tuned tube exhaust headers, parts for both all-out racing and street modifications. But Volvo is no longer in the speed part business. If you're lucky, you'll find some at a swap meet, although they won't be cheap.

Volvos can still be raced successfully. Kurt Omensetter's Werner Motors of Lansdale, Pennsylvania, sponsored this 1971 142E in SCCA's Improved Touring series, here kicking up some spray at Summit Point Raceway in April 1992. *Ray Parsons*

A race-prepped 240 Turbo in action in the European Touring Championship and bearing number 1 from its championship-winning 1985 season. *Volvo*

117

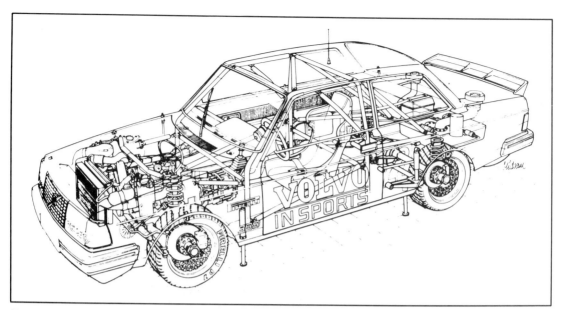

Skeleton view of the 1985 European Touring Championship winning 240 Turbo. Based on a 2141cc B21ET engine with Garrett turbocharger and intercooler, the 1,035kg (2,287lb) racer produced 320hp at 6000rpm and 400lb-ft or torque at 4000-6000rpm. Top speed was more than 250km/h or 155mph. *Volvo*

Competing successfully in the SCCA's Showroom Stock B class was hardly what Volvo engineers had in mind for the 740 Turbowagen, but that's what John Overton did. A string of top ten finishes and even a couple of poles left sports car and super coupe drivers wondering what they did wrong. *Volvo*

Engines and Transmissions

Volvo Engines by Year, US Specification

Notes: US imports began in 1955. All data before that date refers to European-spec cars. Engine designation (in general) is derived from an alpha B or D (for Benzene, i.e., gasoline, or Diesel), a numeric, for engine displacement, followed by a series identifier.

Year	Engine	CC	Type	CR	Carburetion	Hp@rpm	Torque (lb-ft) @rpm	Trans-mission	Model
1947–50	B4B	1414	I-4	6.5	Carter W0618S	40@3800	N/A	M3	PV444
1950–55	B4B	1414	I-4	6.5	Carter W0618S	44@3800	N/A	M3	PV444B/S–PV444H/HS
1955–57	B4B	1414	I-4	7.3	Carter W0618S	51@4500	N/A	M3	PV444K/KS
1955–57	B14A	1414	I-4	7.8	2 SU	70@5500	N/A	M30	PV444
1957–61	B16B	1582	I-4	8.2	2 SU	85@5500	87@3500	M31	PV444;PV544; 122S
1961–67	B18	1778	I-4	8.5	2 SU	90@5000	105@4000	M40	PV544;122S B18
1961–63	B18	1778	I-4	9.5	2 SU	100@5500	108@4000	M41	P1800 (A,B)
1963–65	B18	1778	I-4	10.0	2 SU	108@5800	110@4000	M41	1800S (D,E)
1966	B18	1780	I-4	10.0	2 SU	108@5800	110@4000	M41	1800S
	B18	1778	I-4		2 SU	90@5000	105@3500	M40, BW35	122S
	B18	1778	I-4	N/A	2 SU	95@5000	N/A	M40	PV544
1967	B18	1778	I-4	10.0	2 SU HS 6	115@6000	112@4000	M41,M41, *BW35	1800S;123GT; 144S*
	B18	1778	I-4	8.7	2 SU HS 6	100@5700	108@3500	M40, BW35	122S
1968	B18	1778	I-4	8.7	2 SU HS 6	100@5700	109@3500	M40,M41, BW35	122S
	B18	1778	I-4	10.0	2 SU H6	115@6000	112@4000	M40,M41, *BW35	1800S;144S*
1969	B20	1986	I-4	9.5	2 Z-S 175 CD-25	118@5800	123@3500	M40, BW35	144S

Year	Engine	CC	Type	CR	Carburetion	Hp@rpm	Torque (lb-ft) @rpm	Transmission	Model
	B20	1986	I-4	9.5	2 Z-S 175 CD-25	118@5800	123@3500	M40,M41	1800S
	B30	2980	I-6	9.2	2 Z-S 175 CD-25	145@5500	163@3000	M400, BW35	164
1970	B20	1986	I-4	9.5	2 Z-S 175 CD-25	118@5800	123@3500	M40, BW35	142;144;145
	B20E	1986	I-4	9.5	Bosch elec inj	130@6000	130@3500	M40,M41	1800E
	B30	2980	I-6	9.2	2 Z-S 175 CD-25	145@5500	163@3000	M400, BW35	164
1971	B20	1986	I-4	9.3	2 SU HIF	118@5800	123@3500	M40, BW35	142;144;145
	B20E	1986	I-4	10.5	Bosch elec inj	130@6000	133@3500	M40,M41	142E
	B20E	1986	I-4	10.5	Bosch elec inj	130@6000	133@3500	M41, BW35	1800E
	B30	2982	I-6	9.3	2 Z-S 175 CD-25	145@5500	163@3000	M400, BW35	164
1972	B20	1986	I-4	8.7	2 SU HIF	97@5500	103@3500	M40, BW35	142;144;145
	B20E	1986	I-4	8.7	Bosch elec inj	107@6000	113@3500	M41, BW35	142E
	B20E	1986	I-4	8.7	Bosch elec inj	107@6000	113@3500	M41, BW35	1800E; 1800ES
	B30	2986	I-6	8.7	2 Z-S CD	120@5000	142@3000	M400, BW35	164
	B30F	2986	I-6	8.7	Bosch elec inj	138@5800	154@2500	M400, BW35	164E
1973	B20E	1986	I-4	8.7	Bosch elec inj	112@6000	115@3500	M40, BW35	142;144;145
	B30F	2979	I-6	8.7	Bosch elec inj	138@5500	154@3500	M410, BW35	164
	B20E	1986	I-4	8.7	Bosch elec inj	112@6000	115@3500	M41, BW35	1800ES
1974	B20E	1986	I-4	8.7	Bosch K-Jet inj	109@6000	115@3500	M40, BW35	142;144;145
	B30F	2979	I-6	8.7	Bosch elec inj	138@5500	154@3500	M410, BW35	164E
1975	B20E	1986	I-4	8.7	Bosch CIS inj	98@6000	110@3500	M40,M41, BW35	242;244;245; 242GL;244GL
	B30F	2978	I-6	8.7	Bosch elec inj	130@5250	150@4000	M410, BW35	164
1976	B21F	2127	I-4	8.5	Bosch CIS inj	102@5200 99@5200	114@2500 (49 State) 114@2500 (California)	M45,M46, BW55	242;244;245; 242DL;244DL
	B27F	2673	V-6	8.2	Bosch CIS inj	125@5500 121@5500 (California)	150@2750 (49 State)	M46, BW55	264GL;265DL
1977	B21F	2127	I-4	8.5	Bosch CIS inj	105@5500 101@5200	114@2500 (49 State) 111@2500 (California)	M45,M46, BW55	242;244;245; 242DL;244DL

120

Year	Engine	CC	Type	CR	Carburetion	Hp@rpm	Torque (lb-ft) @rpm	Transmission	Model
	B27F	2673	V-6	8.2	Bosch CIS inj	127@5500	148@2750	M46, BW55	264GL;265DL
1978	B21F	2127	I-4	8.5	Bosch CIS inj	104@5200	117@2500 (49 State)	M45,M46, BW55	242;242GT; 244GL;245DL
						101@5200	111@2500 (California & GT) (all)		
	B27F	2664	V-6	8.2	Bosch CIS inj	125@5500	150@2750	M46, BW55	262C;264GL; 265GL
1979	B21F	2127	I-4	9.3	Bosch CIS inj	107@5250	117@2500	M45,M46, BW55	242;242GT; 244DL;245DL
						101@5200	111@2500 (California & GT)		
	B27F	2664	V-6	8.8	Bosch CIS inj	127@5500	146@2750	M46, BW55	262C;264GL; 265GL
1980	B21F	2127	I-4	9.3	Bosch CIS inj	107@5250	114@2500	M45,M46, BW55	DL;GL;GT
	B24	2383	I-4	23.0	Bosch mech inj	78@4800	98@2800	M46, BW55	Diesel
	B28F	2849	V-6	8.8	Bosch CIS inj	130@5500	153@2750	M46, BW55	GLE;Coupe
1981	B21F	2127	I-4	9.3	Bosch K-Jet inj	107@5250	114@2500	M46, BW5	DL;GL;GLT
	B24	2383	I-4	23.0	Bosch mech inj	76@4800	98@2800	M46, BW55	Diesel
	B27F	2849	V-6	8.8	Bosch K-Jet inj	130@5500	153@2750	BW55	GLE;Coupe
	B21FT	2127	I-4	7.5	Bosch K-Jet inj	127@5400	150@3750	M46, BW55	GLT Turbo
1982	B21F	2127	I-4	9.3	Bosch K-Jet inj	98@5000	112@3000	M46, AW70	DL; GL
	B21FLH	2127	I-4	9.3	Bosch L-Jet inj	105@5400	119@3000	M46	GLT; some DL in Calif.
	D24	2383	I-4	23.0	Bosch mech inj	78@4800	98@2800	M46, BW55	Diesel
	B21FT	2127	I-4	7.5	Bosch K-Jet inj	127@5400	150@3750	M46, AW71	GLT 2.1 liter Turbo
	B28F	2849	V-6	8.8	Bosch K-Jet inj	130@5500	153@2750	BW55	GLE
1983	B23F	2316	I-4	10.3	Bosch L-Jet inj	111@5400	136@3500	M46	DL;GL 2.3 liter
						114@5400	133@3500	AW70	
	D24	2383	I-4	23.0	Bosch mech inj	78@4800	98@2800	M46, BW55	GL 2.4 liter Diesel
	B21FT	2127	I-4	7.5	Bosch K-Jet inj	127@5400	150@3750	M46, AW70	GLT
	D24TD	2383	I-4	23.0	Bosch mech inj	103@4800	139@2400	M46	760GLE 2.4 liter Turbodiesel
	B28F	2849	V-6	8.8	Bosch L-Jet inj	130@5500	153@2750	AW71	760GLE 2.8 liter
1984	B23F	2316	I-4	10.3	Bosch L-Jet inj	111@5400	136@3500	M46	DL;GL 2.3 liter
						114@5400	133@3500	AW70	

Year	Engine	CC	Type	CR	Carburetion	Hp@rpm	Torque (lb-ft) @rpm	Trans- mission	Model
	D24	2383	I-4	23.0	Bosch mech inj	78@4800	98@2800	M46, BW55	DL;GL 2.4 liter Diesel
	D24T	2383	I-4	23.0	Bosch mech inj	103@4800	139@2400	ZF22L	760GLE 2.3 liter Turbodiesel
	B21FT	2127	I-4	7.5	Bosch K-Jet inj	162@5100	181@3900	M46, AW70	Turbo
	B23FT	2316	I-4	8.7	Bosch LH-Jet inj	157@5300	185@2900	M46, AW70	760GLE 2.3 liter Turbo
	B280F	2849	V-6	8.8	Bosch K-Jet inj	134@5500	159@2750	AW71	760GLE 2.8 liter
1985	B230F	2316	I-4	9.5	Bosch LH-Jet inj	114@5400	136@2750	M46, AW70	DL;GL
								M46, ZF22L	740GLE
	B21FT	2127	I-4	7.5	Bosch K-Jet inj	162@5100	175@3900	M46, AW70	Turbo; 740 Turbo
	B230FT	2316	I-4	8.7	Bosch LH-Jet inj	160@5300	187@2900	M46, AW70	760 Turbo
	B28F	2849	V-6	8.8	Bosch K-Jet inj	134@5500	159@2750	M46, AW70	760GLE
	D24T	2383	I-4	23.0	Bosch dist pump	106@4800	140@2400	ZF22L	760TD
1986	B230F	2316	I-4	9.8	Bosch LH-Jet inj	114@5400	136@2750	M46, AW70	240
								M46, ZF22L	740GLE 2.3 liter
	D24T	2383	I-4	23.0	Bosch dist pump	106@4800	140@2400	ZF22L	740GLE 2.4 liter Turbodiesel
	B230FT	2316	I-4	8.7	Bosch LH-Jet inj	160@5300	187@2900	M46, AW71	740 Turbo; 760 Turbo
	B28F	2849	V-6	8.8	Bosch K-Jet inj	134@5500	159@2750	AW71	760GLE V-6
1987	B230F	2316	I-4	9.8	Bosch LH-Jet inj	114@5400	136@2750	M47, AW70L	240
								M47, ZF22L	740 2.3 liter
	B230FT	2316	I-4	8.7	Bosch LH-Jet inj	160@5300	187@2900	M47, AW71	740 2.3 liter Turbo; 760 2.3 liter Turbo
	B280F	2849	V-6	9.5	Bosch LH-Jet inj	145@5100	173@3750	AW71	760 2.8 liter; 780
1988	B230F	2316	I-4	9.8	Bosch LH-Jet inj	114@5400	136@2750	M47, AW70	240
								ZF22L*, AW70L	740 *(sedans only)
	B230FT	2316	I-4	8.7	Bosch LH-Jet inj	160@5300	187@2900	AW71	740 Turbo; 760 Turbo
	B280F	2849	V-6	9.5	Bosch LH-Jet inj	145@5100	173@3750	AW71	760;780
1989	B230F	2316	I-4	9.8	Bosch LH-Jet inj	114@5400	136@2750	M47, AW70	240DL; 240GL
								M47, AW0L	740GL

Year	Engine	CC	Type	CR	Carburetion	Hp@rpm	Torque (lb-ft) @rpm	Transmission	Model
	B230FT	2316	I-4	8.7	Bosch LH-Jet inj	160@5300	187@2900	M46, AW71	740 Turbo; 760 Turbo
	B230F Turbo+	2316	I-4	8.7	Bosch LH-Jet inj	175@5400	187@2900	AW71	780 Coupe Turbo
	B234F	2316	I-4	10.0	Bosch LH-Jet inj	153@5700	150@4450	M46, AW72L	740GLE
	B280F	2849	I-4	9.5	Bosch LH-Jet inj	144@5100	173@3750	AW71	760GLE; 780 Coupe
1990	B230F	2316	I-4	9.8	Bosch LH-Jet inj	114@5400	136@2750	M47, AW70 / M47, AW70L	240; 240DL / 740; 740GL
	B234F	2316	I-4	10.0	Bosch LH-Jet inj	153@5700	150@4450	M46, AW72L	740GLE sixteen-valve
	B230FT Generation 3	2316	I-4	8.7	Bosch LH-Jet	162@4800	195@3450	M46, AW71	740/760/780 Turbo
	B230FT Generation 3+	2316	I-4	8.7	Bosch LH-Jet inj	188@5100	206@3900	M46, AW71	780 Coupe; 740 Turbo
	B280F	2849	V-6	9.5	Bosch LH-Jet inj	144@5100	173@3750	AW71	760GLE;780
1991	B230F	2316	I-4	9.8	Bosch LH-Jet inj	114@5400	136@2750	M47, AW70 / M47, AW70L	240 / 740
	B234F	2316	I-4	10.1	Bosch LH-Jet inj	153@5700	150@4450	AW72L	940GLE sixteen-valve
	B234FT Generation 3	2316	I-4	8.7	Bosch LH-Jet inj	162@4800	195@3450	M46, AW71	740/940 Turbo; 940SE
	B230FT Generation 3+	2316	I-4	8.7	Bosch LH-Jet inj	188@5100	206@3900	AW71	Coupe
1992	B230F	2316	I-4	9.8	Bosch LH-Jet inj	114@5400	136@2750	M47, AW70 / AW70L	240; 240GL / 740; 940GL
	B230FT Generation 3	2316	I-4	8.7	Bosch LH-Jet inj	162@ 4800	195@3450	AW71	740 Turbo Wagon; 940 Turbo
	B6304F	2922	I-4	10.7	Bosch LH-Jet inj	201@6000	197@4300	AW40	960

Automatic Transmission

Model/Series	Year	Transmission
BW35	1966–75	Borg-Warner, three-speed
BW55	1976–	Borg-Warner, three-speed
AW55	1976–	Aisin-Warner, three-speed
AW70	1982–	Aisin-Warner, four-speed
AW70L	1987–	Aisin-Warner, four-speed, lockup torque converter
AW71	1982–	Aisin-Warner, four-speed, heavy-duty
AW72L	1989–	Aisin-Warner, four-speed, reinforced, lockup torque converter
ZF22L	1984–88	Zahnrad Fabrik, four-speed, lockup torque converter
AW40	1992–	Aisin-Warner, four-speed, electronic mode selection

Manual Transmissions

Model/Series	Year	Transmission
M30	–1959	Volvo, three-speed
M31	–1959	Volvo, three-speed with overdrive
M40	1960–75	Volvo, four-speed
M41	1960–75	Volvo, four-speed with overdrive
M400	1969–75	Volvo, four-speed for B30 engine
M410	1969–75	Volvo, four-speed with overdrive for B30 engine
M45	1976–	Volvo, four-speed
M46	1976–	Volvo, four-speed with overdrive
M47	1987–	Volvo, five-speed

Lambda Sond System

Despite the intimidating name, the Volvo Lambda Sond system simply refers to the oxygen sensor in the exhaust system that reads the oxygen in the exhaust.

An electronic control unit—a microprocessor that, as with all computer products, has become evermore micro—calculates the proper air-fuel ratio and then transmits an appropriate command to the airflow sensor and fuel distributor, which adjust the air-fuel mixture. Maintaining the proper ratio allows Volvo to meet emission requirements with a three-way catalyst and without an air pump, thereby getting better fuel economy and power output with less parasitic drag on the engine.

On pre-1986 cars, Volvo recommended that the oxygen sensors be changed at 30,000 miles. For 1986 and thereafter, Volvo says that the sensor should be changed only if it is not working properly.

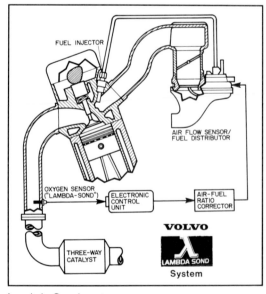

Lambda Sond system.

Volvo Literature

Volvo 1927–1991, Volvo Car Corporation Public Relations & Public Affairs—Softbound, 93 pages, black and white photos

Outline of Volvo history highlights year by year with a PR slant. "Information Section," an appendix, lists limited specifications and statistics. Interesting, although difficult to reconcile for US models for later years.

Bjorn-Eric Lindh, *Volvo—Cars from the 20s to the 90s*, Forlagshuset Norden AB, Malmo, Sweden

Extensive and exhaustive history of Volvo and a reference every Volvo collector should own. However, the book is written from a Swedish perspective and US versions get something less than full treatment.

Bill L. Webb, *Swedish Iron/Volvo 1800*, published by the author

A must for every 1800 owner; lots of valuable restoration tips from one who's been there.

Quick Reference Parts, Volvo North America Corporation, 1991

You don't need this unless you own an independent Volvo repair facility, but if you want a *complete* Volvo library. . . .

Selling Volvo 1956–1986, Brooklands Books

Ads on everything from the PV444 on up to 1986. A good source of information as well as company outlook.

Brooklands Books—Reprints from magazines of road tests and articles on Volvos; you don't have to scour back issues or spend hours digging at flea markets for that old Volvo story you want—unless that's your thing. In addition to *Selling Volvo*, there's:
Volvo 120 Series 1956–1970
Volvo 1800 1956–1970
Road & Track *on Volvo 1957–1975*
Road & Track *on Volvo 1975–1985*
Car and Driver *on Volvo 1955–1986*

Paddock, Lowell, "Sport, Style, and Speed: A History of the Volvo 1800," article, *Automobile Quarterly*, Volume 22, No. 4

A nine-page history of the 1800 series, including the P1900. A well-written addition to your Volvo library, typical *AQ* quality.

Olsson, Christer, *Volvo: Sixty Years of Truckmaking*

The name says it all. If you need to know everything about Volvo, here's 224 pages of trucks from small to large, plus tanks, armored vehicles, and fire engines. Hardbound.

Special Interest Autos No. 94

Eight pages on 1972 Volvo 1800E.

Clubs and Sources

Clubs

Volvo Club of America
PO Box 16
Afton, NY 13730

For owners of Volvos of all models and years, national. Newsletter, parts discounts, technical information, local and national meets.

Volvo Owners' Club
34 Lyonsgate Drive
Downsview, Ontario, Canada M3H 1C8

Canadian/international club with members in Canada, Europe, Brazil, Australia, South Africa, and the United States. Supports members with information and technical support for Volvos of all years, bimonthly newsletter, two annual meets in Canada, local chapters.

Volvo Sports America 1800
1203 W. Cheltenham Avenue
Melrose Park, PA 19126

International club dedicated to the Volvo 1800 Series and other classic Volvos. Technical advice, parts and service discounts, national meets, local chapters, bimonthly magazine.

Washington Volvo Club, Incorporated
5300 Yorktown Road
Bethesda, MD 20816

Despite its name, an international club, "members from California to Maine, Sweden to Puerto Rico." Monthly newsletter.

The Volvo Club of America, Volvo Sports America 1800, and the Washington Volvo Club, Incorporated, combined for the first time in 1991 to hold a joint national meet, many members belonging to one or more of the clubs. The meet, now an annual event, is the largest collection of Volvo owners and cars in the United States. Activities include a concours, banquet, swap meet, rally, and related activities.

Sources

Automat
225A Park Avenue
Hicksville, New York 11801

Carpet kits for 544, 122S, 1800 coupes, and 140 Series.

Charlton Road Autospares
264 Charlton Road
Kingswood, Bristol, England BS151LS

544, 122, 1800 parts, especially off-road and rallying equipment.

Foreign Autotech
York Road and Sunset Lane
Hatboro, PA 19040

Parts specialist for 1800 Series, new and used body and mechanical parts, reproduced floor pans, frame rails, door skins, armrests, dash caps, and so on.

iPd Company, Incorporated
11744 NE Ainsworth Circle
Portland, OR 97220

Specializes in (among other things) improved performance for Volvos, particularly handling parts: "lots of anti-roll bars," Richard Gordon.

Par International Incorporated
Engine Sales Division
3275 Alum Creek Drive, Suite 100
Columbus, OH 43207

New, not rebuilt, 2.7 liter PVR V-6 engines.